Gender and the Millennium Development Goals

Edited by Caroline Sweetman

The books in Oxfam's *Focus on Gender* series were originally published as single issues of the journal *Gender and Development*, which is published by Oxfam three times a year. It is the only European journal to focus specifically on gender and development issues internationally, to explore the links between gender and development initiatives, and to make the links between theoretical and practical work in this field. For information about subscription rates, please apply to Routledge Publishing, T & F Informa UK Ltd., Sheepen Place, Colchester, Essex, OC3 3LP, UK. Tel: +44 (0) 207 017 5544; Fax: +44 (0) 207 017 5198. In North America, please apply to Routledge Publishing, Taylor and Francis Inc., Customer Services Department, 325 Chestnut Street, 8th Floor, Philadelphia, PA 19106, USA; Fax +1 800 821 8312.

journal.orders@tandf.co.uk
www.tandf.co.uk/journals

The views expressed in this book are those of the individual contributors, and not necessarily those of the Editor or the Publisher.

Front cover: *Girls at Lovea Cluster Satellite School, Cambodia, funded by Oxfam.*
Photo: *Howard Davies/Oxfam*

First published by Oxfam GB in 2005

This edition transferred to print-on-demand in 2007

© Oxfam GB 2005

ISBN 0 85598 550 X

A catalogue record for this publication is available from the British Library.

Available from:
Bournemouth English Book Centre, PO Box 1496, Parkstone, Dorset, BH12 3YD, UK
tel: +44 (0)1202 712933; fax: +44 (0)1202 712930; email: oxfam@bebc.co.uk

USA: Stylus Publishing LLC, PO Box 605, Herndon, VA 20172-0605, USA
tel: +1 (0)703 661 1581; fax: +1 (0)703 661 1547; email: styluspub@aol.com

For details of local agents and representatives in other countries, consult our website:
www.oxfam.org.uk/publications
or contact Oxfam Publishing, Oxfam House, John Smith Drive, Cowley, Oxford, OX4 2JY, UK
tel +44 (0) 1865 472255; fax (0) 1865 472393; email: publish@oxfam.org.uk

Our website contains a fully searchable database of all our titles, and facilities for secure on-line ordering.

Published by Oxfam GB, Oxfam House, John Smith Drive, Cowley, Oxford, OX4 2JY, UK

Oxfam GB is a registered charity, no. 202918, and is a member of Oxfam International.

Contents

Editorial

Caroline Sweetman

In 2000, the leaders and heads of state of 189 countries signed the Millennium Declaration, which set a series of targets for global action against poverty by 2015. The Millennium Development Goals (MDGs) are the result of this process. Meeting the MDGs would not end economic poverty; but meeting them could make a positive difference to millions of women, men, and children. In the past decade, 59 countries – predominantly in sub-Saharan Africa and the former Soviet Union – have slid further down the poverty ladder, as they contend with HIV/AIDS, conflict, and enormous foreign debts (UNDP 2004).

In 2005, existing coalitions of activist organisations and individuals will come together in an unprecedented global movement called the Global Call to Action Against Poverty, wearing a white band at key moments during the year to symbolise their demand for immediate action to end poverty. One of the key moments is in September, when the UN Heads of Government will review progress towards the MDGs in New York. The outcome of that meeting will be critical: at current rates of progress, the MDGs are unlikely to be attained by 2015. Only Goal 1, that of halving income poverty, has any chance of being met – but even this achievement is due to progress in a mere handful of countries.

Table 1 sets out the Goals as they were agreed.

Gender issues and the MDGs

This collection of articles focuses on the MDGs from a gender perspective. It examines the strengths and weaknesses of this way of understanding and addressing poverty, and suggests ways of strengthening the approach by using key insights and approaches associated with the 30-year struggle to establish and uphold the rights of women. In 2005, there could potentially be real changes for women living in poverty, and their families. But if this is going to happen, the women's movements in different parts of the world need to believe that the MDGs are part of the solution, rather than part of the problem.

Contributors to this collection come from both sides of this debate. However, ultimately, they all urge gender and

Table 1: The Millennium Development Goals

Goal	1 Eradicate extreme poverty and hunger	2 Achieve universal primary education	3 Promote gender equality and empower women	4 Reduce child mortality	5 Improve maternal health	6 Combat HIV/AIDS, malaria, and other diseases	7 Ensure environ-mental sustainability	8 Develop a global partnership for development
Key targets	Halve the proportion of people living on less than $1 a day by 2015. Halve the proportion of people who suffer from hunger by 2015	Ensure by 2015 that all children complete a full course of primary schooling	Eliminate gender disparity in primary and secondary education by 2005, and in all levels of education by 2015	Reduce the mortality rate of children under five by two-thirds by 2015	Reduce by three-quarters the ratio of women dying in childbirth by 2015	Halt and begin to reverse the incidence of HIV/AIDS and other major diseases by 2015	Halve by 2015 the proportion of people without access to safe drinking water and basic sanitation	Develop a non-discrimi-natory and rules-based trading system, provide more generous aid and deal compre-hensively with the debt problem

development workers and feminist activists to engage with efforts to attain the MDGs by 2015. Contributors here point to the hazards of restricting action to the current priorities set out in the MDG framework, if women's full human rights are to be served and supported by the approach. The alternative path suggested here is to analyse and address the shortcomings of the MDG framework, using insights and analytical tools familiar to feminist activists who have experienced the amazing progress made in the 1990s to establish an international framework of laws, agreements, and pledges to uphold women's full human rights.

Step one – of analysing the MDG framework as it currently stands – is already well advanced. The first issue is the limited 'fit' between the understandings of poverty underpinning the MDGs, and the reality of economic want linked to social and political inequality, as experienced by women. At present, the MDG approach to poverty is charged by feminists with failure to understand and address the gender-specific aspects of women's experience of poverty. Decades of research and activism focusing on the experience of women in poverty have demonstrated that this is as much about agency compromised by abuse, stress, fatigue, and voicelessness as it is about lack of resources. Solving material poverty is not possible for women who lack the power to challenge the discriminatory policies of social institutions, ranging from the family to the state.

Strengths

Supporters of the MDGs argue, first, that one extremely important advance in the approach is that the issue of gender inequality is addressed in Goal 3, aiming to attain gender equality and the empowerment of women. The fact that there is a goal on gender equality and the empowerment of women at all is seen by some as a powerful symbol of the success of the international feminist movement on international politics and development (for example, Subrahmanian 2004). Second, they argue that it is not true to say that the MDGs are informed by an understanding of poverty as purely economic in nature, since the goals place so much stress on social goods such as education and health care.

Another strength of the MDGs is the focus on maternal mortality. Ninety-nine per cent of all maternal deaths occur in the developing world (Freedman 2003, 99). In sub-Saharan Africa, the lifetime risk of a woman dying from pregnancy-related causes is 1 in 16; maternal mortality is higher there than in any other region of the world and reaches 1 in 12 in East and West Africa (Panos 2005). Lynn Freedman points out that the health-care systems in high-mortality countries are 'grossly deficient' (2003, 100).

The MDGs also provide a common conceptual framework and language for the work of governments, UN agencies, international financial institutions, and development organisations from civil society. Although the indicators and targets are inadequate in capturing the full reality of the experience of poverty for women, progress towards them can at least be measured. The framework also potentially provides an opportunity to assess what is preventing particular Goals from being attained. The high profile that the MDGs enjoy means that they provide an opportunity for civil society organisations to hold donors and governments accountable for their failures to provide resources to achieve them.

Weaknesses

Nevertheless, the MDGs do undeniably fail to address social and political margin-alisation where these are not linked to economic want. Hence, they are not useful in supporting women whose security and human dignity are compromised in contexts that are not needy in an economic sense. In his article, presenting a case study of the position of women in Belize, Robert Johnson reminds us of the need for context-specific analysis of the empowerment of women. Targets and indicators may indicate that empowerment of women has occurred, yet the real picture may be very different. Another warning that the MDGs are necessary but not sufficient to address gender-equality concerns comes from Sheila Aikman and Elaine Unterhalter. Their discussion focuses on the gender issues in education that remain after access to education is achieved for girls. Access is the first part of a more complex web of gender issues which affect the teaching and content of education, and are critical determinants of the worth of the education that girls receive.

It is also a fact that the MDGs are silent on violations of women's human rights, including gender-based violence, and are silent on the need to uphold women's reproductive and sexual rights. (The latter are, obviously, not only important in their own right, but critically important if Goal 6, on HIV/AIDS, is to be met.) As Carol Barton explains in her article, the UN Millennium Summit occurred at the end of 25 years of international progress on women's rights, based on the documents that emerged from UN conferences: notably the Beijing Platform for Action (1995) and the Cairo Programme of Action (the output of the UN International Conference on Population and Development in 1994). At the time of the UN Millennium Summit, many feminist activists were fighting to defend the Beijing and Cairo documents from being damaged by right-wing opposition to the hard-won victories on women's rights: in particular, to their reproductive and sexual rights.

It was only when the MDGs were announced at the UN that women's groups discovered that gender equality was relegated to one quite limited Goal, and that the issue of reproductive rights had vanished. The fact that these essential issues were left out, and gender concerns have not been included in other Goals, despite their key relevance, reflects a tendency in international development circles to depoliticise gender issues. There is a widely noted tendency to adopt an integrationist approach to 'mainstreaming' gender concerns, in which they are added to a pre-existing analysis and agenda (Jahan 1995). This failure to allow gender issues to inform and shape the analysis and agenda results in gender issues being collapsed 'within the wider category of poverty' (Subrahmanian 2004, 11), resulting in 'a fairly depoliticised and needs-based discourse [which] … require[s] focus on women within poor households, rather than gender disadvantage per se' (ibid.).

Improving on the MDGs

In development circles, it cannot be taken for granted that all agree on the rationale for challenging gender inequality. Instead, it has often needed to be argued carefully. In order to convince policy-makers to take feminist goals seriously, a synergy must be demonstrated between these and the 'official development priorities' (Kabeer 1999, 435) of national economic development and grassroots poverty alleviation. For example, in her article, Peggy Antrobus points out the need to uphold women's sexual rights if Goal 6, on combating HIV/AIDS, is to be attained.

How can the MDGs be made as useful as possible to women? In their articles, Ceri Hayes and Genevieve Painter consider how the MDG processes and outcome can be strengthened immensely by learning from women's activism, and in particular from the Convention on the Elimination of All Forms of Discrimination Against Women (CEDAW) (UN 1979) and the Beijing Platform for Action. If a rights-based approach is taken to the MDGs, they become a potentially useful route to attaining the vision of gender equality and the empowerment of women that lay at the heart of the Beijing document.

In her article, Ceri Hayes cites some of the advances that have been made at national and international levels to address the inadequacies of the MDG framework. She cites the UN Millennium Project's Task Force on Education and Gender Equality, which has recommended six improvements for Goal 3, including a guarantee of sexual and reproductive health rights for girls and women, and a guarantee of an end to violence against women. Ceri Hayes also outlines some of the practical ways in which human rights principles, and the provisions set out in CEDAW in particular, can be used

to ensure that the MDGs are met in a way that respects and promotes gender equality and women's human rights.

Genevieve Painter's article, written on behalf of the UK-based Gender and Development Network, also urges development workers to give support in 2005 to efforts on the part of the women's movement to reform the MDGs by integrating perspectives, and methods of implementation, suggested by the rights-based approach of the Beijing Platform for Action and CEDAW. In her view, the MDG framework is, therefore, a potentially useful tool for lobbyists to employ in attacks on economic-austerity policies. It is undeniable that the rights-based language of the visionary Millennium Declaration was lost from the MDG framework; yet implementing the MDGs would reflect a commitment to the rights of citizens to demand basic public goods from the state. In this light, the MDG process and framework contain much that is useful for women.

Gaining clarity on women's empowerment: what is it, and how is it attained?

A key criticism of the MDGs from a gender perspective is that the view of the empowerment of women that it includes is a limited one. Naila Kabeer suggests that 'the vision and values of women's groups and organisations across the world have been translated into a series of technical goals to be largely implemented by the very actors and institutions that have blocked their realisation in the past' (this issue).

In recent years, the empowerment of women has become a phrase which means many things to many people. One critic of microfinance interventions that promise empowerment as their result has observed: 'The attractiveness of the concept of empowerment lies mainly in the fact that it legitimises various policies and practices. Empowerment is economically, politically and socially useful' (Lairap-Fonderson 2002, 184).

In her article, Naila Kabeer sets out a feminist model of the empowerment of women, which clearly demonstrates the paralysing effect of economic want on women's agency to challenge inequality. However, this is not to say that addressing economic poverty will result in women 'solving' the issue of structural inequality for themselves. Resources needed to promote the empowerment of women as a sex include, but are not limited to, financial resources.

Money is described as 'frozen desire' (Buchanan 1997, quoted in Oseen 1999, 103), enabling women to enact their own decisions, free from interference by outside actors. To an extent, even if wider society dislikes the idea of independent women, possessing enough money allows one to live free from interference. Yet, obviously, money alone does not make for empowerment. Other resources needed include less tangible goods. These include self-confidence and pride in one's own worth, and knowledge and skills acquired through formal and informal means. Very importantly, resources also include the time and freedom to form strong relationships with other women, which can form a counterpart to the traditional power of the family and marriage in women's lives. Only through spending time together in reflection and discussion do women come to a point where they choose to advance their shared interests. Further, if grassroots action is to shift up a gear to effect structural change for women in society, women need to have the chance to participate in political life at higher levels of society also.

In relation to the MDG process, Kabeer states that it is critical for women to feel a sense of entitlement as citizens if the MDGs are to deliver: 'It is only through the mobilisation of women, particularly poor women, who are primary stakeholders in all of the MDGs, but particularly the MDG on women's empowerment, that policy makers can be held accountable to ensure that the MDGs are followed through in the spirit of the various international movements and meetings that gave rise to them' (this issue).

The MDGs, the state, and citizenship: a help or a hindrance?

A number of articles in this issue consider the question of whether the intellectual vision informing the MDGs is in line with, or inherently opposed to, neo-liberal development models.

To support the first view, Peggy Antrobus considers the MDGs as conforming to the development agendas of the past 20 years, which have damaged individual women, their families, and wider society. A similar view is expressed by Carol Barton, who in her article suggests that the emphasis on the role of the state in the MDGs is confined to ensuring that the state can pave the way for international capital to operate securely. Genevieve Painter argues in her article that the MDGs 'reflect problems in the dominant development approach. They seek to use women in their existing social roles to "deliver" other aims, and do not address the need to eradicate gender inequality, resulting in lack of commitment to address key issues for women, including gender-based violence' (this issue).

This view of the MDGs is coloured by memories of the appalling social impact on women, men, and their families of the Structural Adjustment Policies (SAPs) of the 1980s and 1990s, which exploited women's labour to shore up the negative social impact of adjustment (Elson 1991). Memories of these are still vivid, since, in many contexts, similar policies continue to run. Even Poverty Reduction Strategy Papers (PRSPs), with their promise of participation of women and people in poverty, have failed to live up to the rhetoric with which they were introduced: women's participation has been very patchy, and gender concerns have tended to slip off the agenda (Whitehead and Lockwood 1999, Zuckerman 2002).

However, Genevieve Painter takes a very different line, suggesting in her article that the MDGs are 'shaking the pillars of the growth-driven model of development' (this issue). The focus in the MDGs on social services, including health and education, suggests clearly that the MDGs provide a potential tool with which to challenge austerity spending.

In her article, Arabella Fraser points out that international financing of aid, under Goal 8 of the MDGs, is essential to attaining Goal 5, of improving maternal health. She argues: 'Finance is a necessary, but not sufficient, condition for change to the lives of millions of women who suffer as a result of pregnancy and childbirth – and it is sorely lacking. This is no argument for technical quick-fixes, however. International efforts to reduce maternal mortality must concentrate on improving health systems – a project that entails rebuilding states to deliver services – but must also look to an advocacy grounded in women's rights, as articulated in the Beijing Platform for Action and the Cairo process' (this issue).

Conclusion: the way forward

This collection of articles aims not only to provide readers with information on the debates on gender in relation to the MDGs, but aims to inspire them to action. At the time of going to press, the 49th session of the Commission on the Status of Women (CSW) in New York is about to commence. As Genevieve Painter discusses in her article, there will be a formal link between the review of the Beijing Platform for Action, which will take place at the CSW, and the review of the Millennium Declaration and the MDGs, which will take place in September 2005. There is a risk that fundamentalists may challenge some of the hard-won rights of women at Beijing+10, in particular their sexual and reproductive rights, and women's human rights activists are prepared to

defend these key areas of concern and to ensure that the outcome of the CSW is as robust as possible. Advocacy by activists at the CSW will directly affect the MDG discussions and content. The outcome of the CSW will be transmitted, via the Economic and Social Council of the General Assembly (ECOSOC), to the high-level General Assembly meeting that will review the Millennium Declaration in September 2005.

Both Ceri Hayes' and Genevieve Painter's articles provide guidance and ideas on ways in which activists can work to ensure that women's human rights perspectives are addressed in the MDGs. The UK Gender and Development Network, for example, will focus all its lobbying and advocacy work in 2005 on both the MDG and the Beijing+10 reviews.

Finally, all can participate in the advocacy around the MDG Review. As noted earlier, the Global Call to Action against Poverty is a worldwide alliance committed to ensuring that world leaders live up to their promises to support countries worldwide to meet the MDGs (see www.whiteband.org). For readers in the UK, 'Make Poverty History' is the UK element of the global campaign, consisting of a unique alliance of charities, trade unions, campaigning groups, faith communities, and high-profile individuals who are uniting to tackle global poverty in 2005 (www.oxfam.org.uk/what_you_can_do/campaign/mdg/mph.htm).

References

Beijing Platform for Action (1995) 'The United Nations Beijing Declaration and Platform for Action', www.un.org/womenwatch/daw/beijing/platform/ (last checked 25 February 2005)

Elson, D. (ed.) (1991) *Male Bias in the Development Process*, Manchester: Manchester University Press

Freedman, L. (2003) 'Strategic advocacy and maternal mortality: moving targets and the

8

millennium development goals', *Gender and Development* 11(1): 97–108

Jahan, R. (1995) *The Elusive Agenda: Mainstreaming Women in Development*, London: Zed Books

Kabeer, N. (1999) 'Resources, agency, achievements: reflections on the measurement of women's empowerment', *Development and Change* 30: 435–64

Lairap-Fonderson, J. (2002) 'The disciplinary power of micro credit: examples from Kenya and Cameroon', in J. Parpart, S. Rai, and K. Staudt (eds.) *Rethinking Empowerment: Gender and Development in a Global/Local World*, New York: Routledge

Oseen, C. (1999) 'Women organizing for change: transformational organizing as a strategy for feminist development', in Marilyn Porter and Ellen Judd (eds.) *Feminists Doing Development: A Practical Critique*, London: Zed Books

Panos (2005) 'Safe Motherhood: A Human Rights Perspective', www.panos.org.uk/ global/projectdetails.asp?ProjectID=1017&ID=1 005 (last checked 22 February 2005)

Subrahmanian, R. (2004) 'Promoting gender equality', in Richard Black and Howard White (eds.) *Targeting Development: Critical Perspectives on the Millennium Development Goals*, London: Routledge

UN (1979) 'Convention on the Elimination of All Forms of Discrimination Against Women', www.un.org/womenwatch/ daw/cedaw/ (last checked 2 March 2005)

UNDP (2004) *Human Development Report*, New York: UNDP

Whitehead, A. and M. Lockwood (1999) 'Gender in the World Bank's Poverty Assessments: Six Case Studies from Sub-Saharan Africa', United Nations Research Institute for Social Development (UNRISD) Discussion Paper No. 99, Geneva: UNRISD

Zuckerman, E. (2002) ' "Engendering" Poverty Reduction Strategy Papers (PRSPs): the issues and the challenges', *Gender and Development* 10(3): 88–94

Making the links: women's rights and empowerment are key to achieving the Millennium Development Goals[1]

Noeleen Heyzer

Men and women have the right to live their lives and raise their children in dignity, free from hunger and from fear of violence, oppression or injustice.

Millennium Declaration (UN 2000a, 2)

The Millennium Declaration, adopted by all UN Member States in 2000, outlines a vision of freedom from want and freedom from fear. Together with the eight Millennium Development Goals (MDGs), which make that vision concrete, the Millennium Declaration commits states to 'promote gender equality and the empowerment of women as effective ways to combat poverty, hunger, disease and to stimulate development that is truly sustainable' (UN 2000a, 5).

The recognition that women's equality and rights are central to achieving economic and social priorities is important. But it is not by chance that this has come about. It is the result of work by women's human rights advocates over decades, creating a groundswell of activism for gender equality at global, regional, and national levels. The commitments to women made in the UN World Conferences of the past two decades – in Beijing, Cairo, Vienna, and Copenhagen, as well as the Special Session on HIV/AIDS in New York in June 2001 – are fundamental to the vision embedded in the Millennium Declaration and the MDGs.

So, too, is the UN Convention on the Elimination of All Forms of Discrimination Against Women (CEDAW), an international women's bill of rights – now ratified by 179 countries – which obligates governments to take actions to promote and protect the rights of women (UN 1979). It is crucially important that the specific and detailed commitments and obligations contained in these documents are not lost as governments and the international community begin to organise around goals and targets selected to track progress on the MDGs.

The power of the MDGs lies in the unprecedented global consensus and commitment that they represent. They establish a common index of progress, and a common focus for global partnership for development, which emphasise the needs of poor people. The MDGs also provide an opportunity to raise awareness about the connections among the eight Goals and the rights and capacities of women. The year 2005, which will mark the ten-year review of the Beijing Platform for Action and the five-year review of the Millennium Declaration, will present an opportunity to assess progress in implementing both the

Platform for Action and the MDGs, especially Goal 3.

As governments and civil society come together to track progress towards achieving the MDGs, we have an opportunity to re-energise gender-equality initiatives, by insisting on the central importance of Goal 3 and the Millennium Declaration itself. As a recent World Bank report notes: 'Because the MDGs are mutually reinforcing, progress towards one goal affects progress towards others. Success in many of the goals will have positive impacts on gender equality, just as progress toward gender equality will help other goals' (World Bank Gender and Development Group 2003, 3). It is thus absolutely essential to ensure that tracking progress towards all of the eight Goals relies on sex-disaggregated data and gender-sensitive indicators. Many agencies and advocates for gender equality are producing reports that will contribute to under-standing the gender dimensions of many of the goals and targets.

Progress, however, will again depend on the energy and commitment of women. How then, do women's equality advocates view the MDGs? In order to find out, the United Nations Development Fund for Women (UNIFEM), in co-operation with the UN Interagency Network on Women and Gender Equality, the OECD/DAC Network on Gender Equality, and the Multilateral Development Bank Working Group on Gender, hosted a five-week online discussion on gender and the MDGs with mare than 400 women's equality advocates, representing UN agencies, bilateral donors, multilateral development banks, and civil society organisations, as well as independent scholars and activists. What did this tell us?

First, women's advocates are dismayed that, despite their success in pushing for recognition of women's rights as human rights by governments through UN conferences, many of these hard-won victories are not reaffirmed in the Millennium Declaration, and are entirely absent in the MDGs themselves. They point to the lack of a goal on reproductive rights, or a decent work standard for women or men, the absence of issues such as violence against women, and the narrow targets and indicators for the gender equality goal.

As a result, many women's advocates have questioned the relevance of the MDGs to their work. Why should women's organisations pay attention to the MDGs when the need to tackle the roll-back in women's reproductive rights, the persistence of violence against women, and the rise in militarisms, extremisms, poverty, and inequality is so urgent? Especially when, at face value, the MDGs are operational and are devoid of any analysis of power relations. Nor do they take into account the inequities within the global economic system that exacerbate existing inequalities.

Several participants in the online discussion observed that, in much of the work on MDGs, the gender dimensions were often missing or treated as an afterthought. As one said: 'We have been witness to serious exclusions of a gender perspective in MDG Task Forces, MDG Reports and PRSPs [Poverty Reduction Strategy Papers]. This is just one symptom of a larger epidemic, that puts gender and human rights on a back burner.'

This has begun to change over the last year, as gender advocates made themselves heard in the Task Forces working on strategies for achieving the Goals, and in the statistical agencies working on better data and indicators for monitoring progress. States are already under formal, legal obligations to realise gender equality, particularly those states that have ratified CEDAW. For every area covered by the MDGs, there is direction on gender equality that exists in the core human rights treaties, and through the concluding observations and recommendations of the treaty bodies and special rapporteurs this direction has in many cases already been fine-tuned to the circumstances of individual countries. And, while CEDAW is not fully reflected in the formulation of the MDGs, the Millennium Declaration itself reaffirms a global commitment to implement the Convention.

Progress in implementing these agreements, however, has highlighted some of the obstacles to be overcome in achieving Goal 3. The five-year review of progress in implementing the Beijing Platform, held in June 2000, showed that the path had been bumpy at best. As the Secretary-General's report states: 'an improved understanding of gender equality does not necessarily automatically translate into gender equality in practice. Despite progress, the persistence of traditional and stereotypic gender roles, often reinforced by legal and/or institutional structures, impedes women's empowerment. Promotion of gender equality continues to be relegated to a lower level of national priority' (UN 2000b, 10). The result of this is that resources are often in short supply.

This uneven progress results from a complex set of conditions that lie at the heart of women's inequality. The structures that perpetuate gender inequality and discrimination pervade economic, social, political, cultural, legal, and civic institutions, norms, and practices around the world. The know-how and investments required to eliminate them are rarely committed, especially in poor countries. The political will required to achieve gender equality is variable, or altogether lacking. Although positive actions have been taken in almost every country, the Secretary-General's report concludes that 'more work needs to be done, at every level, to create the enabling environment envisioned in the Platform for Action, in which women's rights are recognized as an indispensable part of human rights and women as well as men have the opportunity to realize their full potential' (ibid. 10–11).

What will it take?

Making gender equality and women's human rights central to the MDGs means making connections between the MDGs and global agreements such as CEDAW and those that emerged from Vienna, Beijing, and Cairo. This requires a commitment from donors to finance women's empowerment. It requires support for women's organising, to push for policies to ensure that rhetoric is translated into concrete actions. And finally, it requires recognition by the international development community that the motor of gender mainstreaming is commitment to women's rights and gender empowerment.

For this reason, we must guard against falling into a kind of technocratic approach to gender mainstreaming that governments and agencies can adopt, without actually talking to women – particularly women who are poor and disadvantaged. We must guard against regarding gender equality and women's empowerment as a set of technical tools and concepts de-linked from practice, power, and politics. This is because, in the last analysis, all of these are necessary to build the vital partnerships needed to fulfil our commitments to the world's women. What women are telling us is that they need to believe in the rhetoric. In the words of one participant in our study: 'Women, and the poor in general, have suffered too much from economic recycling and broken promises. Women have reason to be very skeptical about cooptation, and attempts to use them as an excuse to push an agenda that is not theirs. We must make sure that agenda setting is not done without concern for our voices and warnings.'

The MDGs may represent another chance – perhaps the only one – to heed these voices and to link the goals and aspirations of women to the priorities of governments and development specialists. Achieving the Goals demands that we find a way to mobilise the political will and the financial resources to turn rhetoric into action.

Noeleen Heyzer is Executive Director of UNIFEM.

Note

1 This article is taken from an address originally given at the Workshop on Gender Equality and the Millennium Development Goals, World Bank, Washington DC, on 19 November 2003. Since the article was written, many of the links the author that laid out have been codified in detail in a UNIFEM booklet (2004).

References

UN (1979) 'Convention on the Elimination of All Forms of Discrimination Against Women', 1249 UNTS 13, www.un.org/ womenwatch/daw/cedaw/ (last checked March 2005)

UN (2000a) 'United Nations Millennium Declaration', www.un.org/millennium/ declaration/ares552e.pdf (last checked March 2005)

UN (2000b) 'Review and Appraisal of the Implementation of the Beijing Platform for Action: Report of the Secretary-General', www.un.org/womenwatch/ daw/csw/ecn6-2000-pc2.pdf (last checked March 2005)

UNIFEM (2004) *Pathway to Gender Equality: CEDAW, Beijing and the MDGs*, UNIFEM

World Bank Gender and Development Group (2003) 'Gender Equality and the Millennium Development Goals', http://siteresources.worldbank.org/INTGEND ER/Publications/20169280/gendermdg.pdf (last checked March 2005)

Gender equality and women's empowerment:
a critical analysis of the third Millennium Development Goal[1]

Naila Kabeer

This article discusses the third Millennium Development Goal (MDG), on gender equality and women's empowerment. It explores the concept of women's empowerment and highlights ways in which the indicators associated with this Goal – on education, employment, and political participation – can contribute to it.

Gender equality and women's empowerment is the third of eight MDGs. It is an intrinsic rather than an instrumental goal, explicitly valued as an end in itself rather than as an instrument for achieving other goals. Important as education is, the translation of this goal into the target of eliminating gender disparities at all levels of education within a given time period is disappointingly narrow. However, the indicators to monitor progress in achieving the goal are somewhat more wide-ranging:

- closing the gender gap in education at all levels;

- increasing women's share of wage employment in the non-agricultural sector;

- and increasing the proportion of seats held by women in national parliaments.

In this article, I interpret this as meaning that each of the three 'resources' implied by these indicators – education, employment, and political participation – is considered essential to the achievement of gender equality and women's empowerment. Each

of these resources certainly has the potential to bring about positive changes in women's lives, but, in each case, it is the social relationships that govern access to the resource in question that will determine the extent to which this potential is realised. Thus, in each case, there is both positive and negative evidence about the impact of women's access to these resources on their lives. There are lessons to be learned from both. The article also considers some of the other 'resources' that have been overlooked by the MDGs, but could be considered equally important for the goal in question.

Conceptualising empowerment: agency, resources, and achievement

First, however, it is important to clarify what is implied by 'empowerment' in this article. One way of thinking about power is in terms of the *ability to make choices*. To be disempowered means to be denied choice, while empowerment refers to the processes by which those who have been denied the ability to make choices acquire such an ability. In other words, *empowerment entails change*. People who exercise a great deal of choice in their lives may be very powerful, but they are not *empowered*, in the sense in which I use the term, because they were never disempowered in the first place.

However, for there to be a real choice, certain conditions must be fulfilled:

- There must be alternatives – the ability to have chosen differently. Poverty and disempowerment generally go hand in hand, because an inability to meet one's basic needs – and the resulting dependence on powerful others to do so – rules out the capacity for meaningful choice. This absence of choice is likely to affect women and men differently, because gender-related inequalities often intensify the effects of poverty.

- Alternatives must not only exist, they must also be *seen* to exist. Power relations are most effective when they are not perceived as such. Gender often operates through the unquestioned acceptance of power. Thus women who, for example, internalise their lesser claim on household resources, or accept violence at the hands of their husbands, do so because to behave otherwise is considered outside the realm of possibility. These forms of behaviour could be said to reflect 'choice', but are really based on the denial of choice.

Not all choices are equally relevant to the definition of power. Some have greater significance than others in terms of their consequences for people's lives. Strategic life choices include where to live, whether and whom to marry, whether to have children, how many children to have, who has custody over children, freedom of movement and association, and so on. These help to frame other choices that may be important for the quality of one's day-to-day life, but do not constitute its defining parameters. Finally, the capacity to exercise strategic choices should not violate this capacity on the part of others.

The concept of empowerment can be explored through three closely interrelated dimensions: agency, resources, and achievements. Agency represents the processes by which choices are made and put into effect. It is hence central to the concept of empowerment. Resources are the medium through which agency is exercised; and achievements refer to the outcomes of agency. Below, each of these dimensions is considered in turn, as is their interrelationship in the context of empowerment.

Agency

Agency has both positive and negative connotations:

- Its positive sense – the 'power to' – refers to people's ability to make and act on their own life choices, even in the face of others' opposition.

- Its negative sense – the 'power over' – refers to the capacity of some actors to override the agency of others through, for example, the exercise of authority or the use of violence and other forms of coercion.

However, as noted earlier, power also operates in the absence of explicit forms of agency. Institutional bias can constrain people's ability to make strategic life choices. Cultural or ideological norms may deny either that inequalities of power exist or that such inequalities are unjust. Subordinate groups are likely to accept, and even collude with, their lot in society, if challenging this either does not appear possible or carries heavy personal and social costs.

Agency in relation to empowerment, therefore, implies not only actively exercising choice, but also doing this in ways that challenge power relations. Because of the significance of beliefs and values in legitimating inequality, a process of empowerment often begins from within. It encompasses not only 'decision making' and other forms of observable action but also the meaning, motivation, and purpose that individuals bring to their actions; that is, their *sense* of agency. Empowerment is rooted in how people see themselves – their sense of self-worth. This in turn is critically bound up with how they are seen by those around them and by their society.

Resources
Resources are the medium through which agency is exercised. They are distributed through the various institutions and relationships in a society. In institutions, certain actors have a privileged position over others concerning how rules, norms, and conventions are interpreted, as well as how they are put into effect. Heads of households, chiefs of tribes, directors of firms, managers of organisations, and elites within a community all have decision-making authority in particular institutions by virtue of their position. The way in which resources are distributed thus depends on the ability to define priorities and enforce claims. Equally importantly, it defines the terms on which resources are made available. If a woman's primary form of access to resources is as a dependent member of the family, her capacity to make strategic choices is likely to be limited.

Achievements
Resources and agency make up people's capabilities: that is, their potential for living the lives they want. The term 'achievements' refers to the extent to which this potential is realised or fails to be realised; that is, to the outcomes of people's efforts. In relation to empowerment, achievements have been considered in terms of both the agency exercised and its consequences. For example, taking up waged work would be regarded by the MDGs as evidence of progress in women's empowerment. However, it would be far more likely to constitute such evidence if work was taken up in response to a new opportunity or in search of greater self-reliance, rather than as a 'distress sale' of labour. It is also far more likely to be empowering if it contributes to women's sense of independence, rather than simply meeting survival needs.

The interrelationship between agency, resources, and achievements
There is a distinction, therefore, between 'passive' forms of agency (action taken when there is little choice), and 'active' agency (purposeful behaviour). There is also a further important distinction between greater 'effectiveness' of agency, and agency that is 'transformative'. The former relates to women's greater efficiency in carrying out their given roles and responsibilities, the latter to their ability to act on the restrictive aspects of these roles and responsibilities in order to challenge them. For example, in India, the reduction of overall child mortality has been associated with rising female literacy. This can be interpreted as the product of 'effective' agency on the part of women in their role as mothers. However, the reduction of gender disparities in under-five mortality rates has transformative implications, because it shows a form of agency that is acting against the grain of patriarchal values, which define daughters as having less worth than sons.

The focus in this article is on transformative forms of agency on the part of women and on those achievements that suggest a greater ability on the part of poor women to question, analyse, and act on the structures of patriarchal constraint in their lives. The three dimensions that make up the concept of empowerment can be seen as representing the pathways through which these processes of empowerment can occur. Changes in any one dimension can lead to changes in others. For instance, 'achievements' in one sphere of life can form the basis on which women seek improvements in other spheres in the future. Policy changes that provide women with access to new 'resources' may be the result of their collective action to achieve this change. Such changes may occur over the life course of an individual or group or across generations, as mothers seek to give their daughters the chances that they themselves never had. The reverse is also true. Inequalities in one sphere are likely to get reproduced in other spheres of society if they go unchallenged. Today's inequalities are translated into the inequalities of tomorrow as daughters inherit the same discriminatory structures that oppressed their mothers.

We are, therefore, interested in transformative forms of agency that do not simply address immediate inequalities but are used to initiate longer-term processes of change in the structures of patriarchy. While changes in the consciousness and agency of individual women are an important starting point for such processes, it will do little on its own to undermine the systemic reproduction of inequality. Institutional transformation requires movement along a number of fronts: from individual to collective agency, from private negotiations to public action, and from the informal sphere to the formal arenas of struggle where power is legitimately exercised. The question then is what the three resources identified by MDG 3 contribute to these movements.

Access to education

The positive effects of education

There is considerable evidence for the claim that access to education can bring about changes in cognitive ability, which is essential to women's capacity to question, to reflect on, and to act on the conditions of their lives and to gain access to knowledge, information, and new ideas that will help them to do so (see review in Jejeebhoy 1995). This is evident in everyday instances. In Kenya, it was found that women with at least four years of schooling were able to correctly understand instructions for administering oral rehydration salts; but only those with at least secondary education were able to explain the environmental causes of diarrhoea. In Nigeria, less educated women were as likely as educated ones to have their children

immunised; educated women were more likely than uneducated ones to know about family planning; but only secondary-schooled women revealed an in-depth understanding about disease and prevention.

Education increases the likelihood that women will look after their own well-being along with that of their family. A study in rural Zimbabwe found that among the factors that increased the likelihood of women accessing contraception and antenatal care – both of which improve maternal survival and well-being – were education and paid work (Becker). In rural Nigeria, 96 per cent of women with secondary and higher education, 53 per cent of those with primary education, and 47 per cent of those with little or no education had sought post-natal care.

There are also other effects associated with education that suggest a change in power relationships within and outside the household. In rural Bangladesh, educated women in rural areas participate in a wider range of decisions than uneducated ones. Whereas the latter participated in an average of 1.1 decisions, the number increased to 1.6, 2.0, and 2.3 among women with primary, middle, and secondary education respectively. A study from Tamil Nadu found that better-educated women scored higher than less educated women on a composite index measuring their access to, and control over, resources, as well as their role in economic decision-making.

Educated women also appear less likely to suffer from domestic violence. A study by Sen in West Bengal noted that educated women were better able to deal with violent husbands: 'access to secondary stages of education may have an important contributory role in enhancing women's capacity to exercise control in their lives ... through a combination of literacy and numeracy skills, and enhanced self-esteem' (Sen 1999, 12). Similar findings were recorded in rural Bangladesh (Schuler et al. 1996).

Education appears to increase women's capacity to deal with the outside world, including government officials and service providers of various kinds. In rural Nigeria, uneducated women preferred not to deliver in hospitals because of the treatment they received at the hands of nurses, a treatment not meted out to the more educated and self-confident women who were surveyed (cited in Jejeebhoy 1995). Finally, the exposure to new ideas can translate into direct collective challenges to male prerogatives. The widely documented anti-liquor movement mounted by members of Mahila Samakhya, a literacy programme for women in India, was sparked off by images of collective action against alcoholism in their literacy primer (Niranjana 2002).

Limits to education as a route to empowerment

However, there are also studies that suggest that the changes associated with education are likely to be conditioned by the context in which it is provided and the social relationships that it embodies and promotes. In societies that are characterised by extreme forms of gender inequality, not only is women's access to education curtailed by various restrictions on their mobility and their limited role in the wider economy, but its effects may also be more limited. Where women's role in society is defined purely in reproductive terms, education is seen in terms of equipping girls to be better wives and mothers, or increasing their chances of getting a suitable husband. These are legitimate aspirations, given the realities of the society. However, they do little to equip girls and women to question the world around them, and the subordinate status assigned to them.

A second set of qualifications concerns the relationships embodied in the delivery of education. Social inequalities are often reproduced through interactions within the school system. In India, for example, not only do the children of poor and scheduled-caste households attend different, and differently resourced, schools, but, even within the same school, different groups of children are treated differently. *Dalit* children are sometimes made to sit separately from others, are verbally abused, are used for running menial errands, and are physically punished more often than higher-caste children. There is also evidence of widespread gender bias, with teachers showing more attention to boys and having a lower opinion of girls' abilities. The absence, or minority presence, of female teachers is a problem in many areas. Reinforcing the male dominance of public services, it can act as a barrier to girls' access to and completion of schooling.

Teachers in Africa also have different attitudes towards male and female students, on the basis that boys need careers and girls need husbands. They tend to be dismissive and discouraging towards girls and to give more classroom time to boys, who are usually more demanding. Even when girls are encouraged to pursue a career, they are expected to opt for the 'caring' professions, in other words teaching and nursing. The 'hidden curriculum' of school practice reinforces messages about girls' inferior status on a daily basis and provides them with a negative learning experience, thus creating a culture of low self-esteem and low aspirations.

The less hidden content of the educational curriculum also mirrors and legitimates wider social inequalities, denigrating physical labour (largely the preserve of poor people) and domestic activities (largely the preserve of women). Gender stereotyping in the curriculum portrays girls as passive, modest, and shy, while boys are seen as assertive, brave, and ambitious. This reinforces traditional gender roles in society, and acts to limit the kinds of futures that girls are able to imagine for themselves. The design of educational curricula has not yet taken account of the fact that many more women are entering the labour market around the world, making critical contributions to household income and frequently heading their own households. Policy makers often continue to see the benefits of educating girls and women in terms of improving family health and welfare, rather than preparing women for a more equal place in the economy and in society. Women's lack of skills partly explains why they continue to be confined to the poorer paid and more casualised forms of paid work.

These limitations to education as a route to empowerment do not negate the earlier positive findings, but they suggest the need for caution in assuming that the effects of education can be taken for granted or that they will be uniform across all contexts. They point to the various aspects of educational provision that militate against not only its empowerment potential but even its ability to attract and retain girls in school, particularly those from poor backgrounds.

Access to paid work

There is also a solid body of evidence to show that access to paid work can increase women's agency in strategic ways.

Positive implications of self-employment
Even paid work carried out in the home has the potential to shift the balance of power within the family. A detailed study of women engaged in industrial homework in Mexico City noted that in households where women's economic contribution was critical to household survival, women had been able to negotiate a greater degree of respect (Benería and Roldán 1987). Studies of the impact of microcredit in societies where women have traditionally been excluded from the cash economy have found that women's access to credit led to a number of positive changes in women's own perceptions of themselves, and their role in household decision making (Kabeer 2001; Kabeer forthcoming). It also led to a long-term reduction in domestic violence, as well as an increase in women's assets. Such effects were stronger when these loans were used to

initiate or expand women's own income-generating activities, despite the fact that these continued to be largely home-based (Hashemi *et al.* 1996; Schuler *et al.* 1996). A recent survey of the impact of various microfinance organisations (MFOs) in India and Bangladesh noted that longer-term membership of such groups also led to various categories of wider impact, including higher levels of political participation, improved access to government programmes, and practical skills, as well as knowledge of the wider society, self-confidence in dealing with public officials, and the likelihood of participating in protests and campaigns (Kabeer, forthcoming). However, the study notes that these impacts depend not only on the provision of financial services of various kinds, but also on the kinds of group that MFOs promote.

Positive implications of wage labour in agriculture
However, the most striking feature of recent decades has been the large-scale entry of women into the labour market across the world: the 'feminisation' of the labour force. The rise of non-traditional agricultural export (NTAE) production in a number of African and Latin American countries has led to a rise in wage employment for women in medium- and large-scale production units. Studies suggest that this income has brought about a number of economic improvements for women themselves and for their families, and show that they exercise a considerable say in how their money is spent (see, for instance, the review in Dolan and Sorby 2003). A study in Ecuador found that more than 80 per cent of women in the flower industry managed their own wages. Among female employees in the Kenyan vegetable industry, single women managed and controlled their own wages, while married women usually managed their incomes jointly with husbands.

There is also significant evidence from the vegetable industries of Guatemala and the Dominican Republic, and the flower industry of Mexico, that women's participation in wage employment has led to greater independence in household decision making. In some cases, as among women working in the fresh vegetable industry in the Dominican Republic, it has allowed them to escape abusive marriages. Women working in the flower industry in Colombia reported widening their social networks in ways that would otherwise have proved difficult in rural areas. Workers in the fresh vegetable industry in Kenya not only reported greater economic independence, but also new opportunities for meeting with women from other parts of the country.

Positive implications of non-agricultural wage labour

Evidence of changes in women's life chances as a result of entry into waged work appears to be more marked when it occurs in the non-agricultural sector (see the review of literature in Kabeer, forthcoming). This is partly because such employment is generally associated with migration by women out of rural areas and away from the patriarchal controls of kinship and community. In a country where women had previously been denied public forms of employment, women workers in the export garment industry in Bangladesh expressed their satisfaction at having a 'proper' job and regular wages, compared with the casual, poorly paid forms of employment that had previously been their only options. Many had used their new-found earning power to renegotiate their relations within marriage, others to leave abusive marriages. Women who had previously not been able to help out their ageing parents once they got married now insisted on their right to do so. Yet others used their earnings to postpone early marriage and to challenge the practice of dowry. In addition, they valued the new social networks that they were able to build with their co-workers, and the greater sense of independence they now enjoyed.

Similarly positive evaluations are reported in a number of other studies. As in Bangladesh, women in Turkey had previously been permitted to work outside the home only if it was necessary for family survival. In a study of the clothing industry, however, many of those interviewed no longer saw their work as subordinate to their familial roles, to be abandoned when they got married or had children. Rather, they saw it as a more permanent way of life. The overwhelming majority had made their own decision to enter factory work, giving as their reasons their desire to make use of their skills and to be outside the home. Forty per cent of the workers, who were mainly young single women, indicated their preference to work a considerable distance from home in order to escape the control exercised by their family and neighbours. They wanted to work somewhere where they could move about freely during their lunch breaks and take the opportunity to meet their friends, including boyfriends.

A study of women workers in export manufacturing jobs in the Philippines found that most of them earned at least as much as – and many earned more than – the legal minimum wage, and they also enjoyed more benefits than in alternative forms of employment. They had the opportunity to delay marriage and childbirth, and the scope for personal independence and self-determination that comes with relatively high wages and relatively stable employment (compared with work in the informal economy). While factory employment may not provide much satisfaction in itself, it was suggested that it could gradually lead to positive changes in women's personal and household circumstances.

In China, young, single women migrate from the countryside to live and work in the export-processing zones in the south. Such jobs are fiercely competed for in the country-side, because they are more remunerative than agricultural work. Moreover, many women previously worked on family farms where they never received an independent wage. Young women wanted to earn money, not only to help their families but also to buy things for themselves without having to account to someone for whatever they spent. Others used their earnings to meet the demand for repayment of bride price or child support by husbands whom they wished to divorce.

In Honduras, women working in *maquiladoras* (assembling manufactured goods for export) earned higher wages than workers elsewhere, and they reported improvements in household relationships and help in domestic work from male members. They were more likely to have voted in elections and more likely to feel that they carried some weight with the government. These trends became stronger over time. This may explain why, while most workers wanted to see improvements, especially in their wages, 96 per cent reported that they were very (49 per cent) or somewhat (47 per cent) satisfied with their jobs. Similarly, married women workers in export-oriented manufacturing factories in a number of Caribbean countries reported improvements in household relations as a result of their greater economic contributions, with greater sharing of decision making with male partners.

The limits to empowerment through paid work

On the other hand, most of these studies also highlight the exploitative conditions of work in which women are generally found. The greatest attention has been paid to women who work in the agro and manufacturing industries, which seek to compete internationally through the promotion of flexible labour practices. Export-oriented manufacturing is associated with extremely long hours of work during busy seasons, often combined with lay-offs in the slack season, and poor conditions. In China, most women from the localities in which these industries are based shunned such work if they could find employment with higher status or that was less tedious. There are also health hazards. *Maquila* workers in

Honduras, for example, were more likely to report a health problem in the previous month than those who had been working elsewhere, and they had less leisure. Studies from Vietnam and Bangladesh both found long hours of work in the same position to be the major source of complaint among women workers in the export sector, together with various ailments associated with this.

Moreover, not all studies report positive findings concerning women's capacity to have greater control over their lives. Many women who leave rural areas to take up jobs in towns, in order to make new friends and build a life for themselves, do not have time to take up such opportunities. The division of labour in domestic chores and child care is rarely renegotiated between the sexes. Despite their increased labour input into paid work, women (particularly married women) either continue to bear the main burden of domestic work, or share it with other female members of the household – often their daughters. By and large, gender inequalities in work burdens appear to be intensified. Despite the collective nature of their work, women workers in these sectors are either forbidden to unionise or find it difficult to do so.

Moreover, despite the visibility of export-oriented waged employment in agriculture and industry, the vast majority of women in low-income countries continue to work in the informal economy in various forms of economic activities that may or may not be affected by global markets, but are characterised by far worse conditions. Within this informal economy, poorer women are concentrated in the most casualised forms of waged labour, and low-value own-account enterprises. It is difficult to see how earnings generated by sex work, domestic service, or daily labour on construction sites – which is where the poorest women are likely to be found – will do much to improve women's subordinate status at home or at work.

Political representation

The last of the indicators for monitoring progress on gender equality and women's empowerment relates to the number of seats held by women in national parliaments. It moves the focus of empowerment into the arena of politics, and the struggle for participation and representation in decision-making structures.

Positive effects of national representation

As half of the population, women are clearly entitled to at least half the seats in parliament. Such an achievement could, with certain qualifications, represent the most ambitious of the three forms of change singled out to measure progress on women's empowerment and could have the greatest potential for transformation. Furthermore, again with certain qualifications, it could potentially address many of the constraints that limit the life chances of poor women.

However, because these qualifications relate to the same constraints that have prevented women from all social classes and groups from having a 'strategic presence' in national parliaments, it is also the form of social change least likely to be achieved in the near future. A review of the relevant statistics suggests that, regardless of political systems, the proportion of women in national parliaments around the world is extremely low, averaging 13.8 per cent in 2000 (Goetz 2003). This is an extraordinary under-representation of women in the highest structures of governance in their countries. Various forms of bias in the institutions of civil society and the political sphere – more so than conscious discrimination – operate to exclude women, including women from privileged elites.

The structure of the political sphere makes a difference to how many women are fielded as candidates and how many win. This includes the extent to which political parties have taken institutional root in society; have clear rules about candidate selection; and identify relevant policy concerns. Most important, is the political culture in which parties operate and the extent to which it is conducive to the promotion of women's involvement in politics: the strength or weakness of patriarchal ideology, the existence of pluralist forms of organisation, the degree of religious opposition to gender reforms.

Electoral systems are also important. The ones more likely to bring women into political office are those where more than one person can represent a constituency; those that have multiple parties competing for votes; and those that practise proportional representation (PR) in party lists.

Those less likely to do so are majoritarian systems which create the incentive to field a single candidate per constituency and appeal to the majority, rather than accommodating diversity. A review of 53 legislatures in 1999 found that national assemblies in PR systems had nearly 24 per cent of women, compared with 11 per cent in majoritarian systems. In almost every case where women exceed 15 per cent of elected representative bodies, this has been the result of special measures that accord positive advantage to female candidates: Mozambique has 30 per cent female parliamentarians, while South Africa has 29 per cent. Bangladesh, Burkina Faso, India, Tanzania, and Uganda all have reserved seats for women in national or local government.

The way that quotas are applied makes a difference to whether the presence of women is 'token' or a legitimate form of representation. Where, as in Bangladesh, women's seats were filled by the party in power, they simply became an additional vote bank for the ruling regime. In South Africa, on the other hand, there have been attempts by the women's movement to encourage members from within their ranks to enter politics. A woman MP there was active in initiating the process of examining national budgets from a gender perspective; and the Women's Budget Initiative, established in

1995, brought together parliamentarians and NGOs to scrutinise the allocation of public resources (Budlender, Hicks, and Vetten 2002).

At the same time, it should be noted that, at present, the women who enter national parliaments are not generally drawn from the ranks of poor people, nor is there any guarantee that they will be more responsive to the needs and priorities of poor women than many men in parliament.

Positive effects of local government

There is some debate about whether greater participation and influence in local government structures are more relevant goals for poor women than increasing women's seats in national parliaments. The former, after all, make the decisions that most directly affect the lives of poor people. In recognition of this, a number of states in India, where there is now 33 per cent reservation of seats for women in local government, have added further induce-ments to local communities to encourage women's participation. Madhya Pradesh and Kerala, for example, require that one-third of participants in the regular open village meetings are female before there is considered to be a quorum. Kerala also allocates 10 per cent of development funds received by local councils from the state to be used for 'women's development' and to be managed by representatives of female groups of the village assembly.

Clearly, all these measures, including the reservation policy itself, are open to abuse. There has been much discussion in India about the possibility that women are merely proxies for husbands or powerful men within their family or caste. Objections are raised on the grounds that only supporters of parties in power attend village meetings; or that women are being harassed to spend funds in ways that do not benefit poorer women. While these are valid concerns, they may also alter over time, as women become more experienced in the political arena. Studies from India, for example, showed that many of the elected women were gaining self-confidence. They questioned the priorities of *panchayat* (local government) development programmes, emphasised issues affecting women such as fuel and water, and had begun to build broad alliances among themselves. One study showed that women representatives were likely to allocate resources differently from men, suggesting that their presence allowed a different set of priorities to be expressed.

Building citizenship from the grassroots

It is clear that each of the resources in question had the potential to bring about the kinds of change that could lead to renegotiations of the boundaries between public and private life, to collective forms of struggle, and to women's greater represent-ation in the structures of decision making. Together, they could also provide the basis on which women could organise to address the other aspects of the patriarchal structures on which the MDGs are silent: reproductive rights, violence against women, unjust laws, and so on. However, it is also clear that there are likely to be powerful forces, some within the policy domain itself, that will militate against this happening. It is only through the mobilisation of women, particularly poor women, who are primary stakeholders in all of the MDGs, but particularly the MDG on women's empowerment, that policy makers can be held accountable to ensure that the MDGs are followed through in the spirit of the international movements and meetings that gave rise to them. Yet it is precisely this that is missing from the letter and spirit of the MDGs. The vision and values of women's groups and organisations across the world have been translated into a series of technical goals, to be implemented mainly by the very actors and institutions that have blocked their realisation in the past.

If the vision and values that gave rise to the demand for gender equality and women's empowerment in the first place are to be restored to MDG 3, then those with most at stake in its implementation in accordance with this spirit must be in a position to participate in the processes by which it is translated into objectives, activities, and outcomes. This is most likely to happen if the women in question, together with their allies in government and civil society, are mobilised to participate in these processes. Sometimes such mobilisations have begun to occur because of the nature of certain activities. We have noted the way in which microfinance can provide the basis for building women's capacity for collective action. We have also noted how such action can spill over into the political sphere, not simply in the form of voting, but also in interactions with locally represented officials and participation in protests. We are also seeing evidence of greater willingness on the part of women workers to challenge their employers and the state through organisations such as SEWA (Self-Employed Women's Association) and Mahila Samakhya in India, and Kormojibi Nari and Nijera Kori in Bangladesh. We have seen the innovation of Women's Budget Initiatives in a number of countries, not simply as a technical exercise but as a way of learning more about how governance structures function and how resources are raised and allocated. It is through the mobilisation of women as women but also as workers, mothers, and citizens that the international community can ensure that the MDGs speak to the needs and interests of half of the world's population. Building this collective capacity of women in all spheres of life to participate and to hold authorities accountable is thus the only basis on which the world's policy makers can keep the promises that they have made on the issue of gender equality.

Conclusion

Gender relations, like all social relations, are multi-stranded: they embody ideas, values, and identities; they allocate labour between different tasks, activities, and domains; they determine the distribution of resources; and they assign authority, agency, and decision-making power. This means that gender inequalities are multi-dimensional and cannot be reduced to some single and universally agreed set of priorities. Any attempt to do so will run the danger of being either too narrow (as the MDGs have been accused of being) or a wish list that is too long and complex to act on. However, gender relationships are not internally cohesive. They contain contradictions and imbalances, particularly when there have been changes in the wider socio-economic environment. Consequently, a shift in one aspect of social relations can initiate a series of changes in other aspects, with unpredictable consequences. To that extent, it could be argued that each of the three indicators embodied in MDG 3 has the potential to make a difference. Each can bring about immediate changes with longer-term consequences. Indeed, the same could be said of any set of policies that seeks to improve women's access to resources. Some may be more strategic than others, but all have transformatory potential as long as the change in question is a genuine expansion of women's choices, rather than a token gesture of paternalist benevolence.

However, what this article has also argued that unless provision is made to ensure that policy changes are implemented in ways that allow women themselves to participate, to monitor, and to hold policy makers, corporations, and other relevant actors accountable for their actions, this potential is unlikely to be realised. Women's access to education may improve their chances of a good marriage or their capacity to sign their names on a document, but unless it also provides them with the analytical capacity and courage to question unjust practices, its potential for change will be limited. Women's access to paid work may give them a greater sense of self-reliance and greater purchasing power, but if it is undertaken in conditions that erode their health and exploit their labour, its costs may outweigh its benefits. Women's presence in the governance structures of society clearly carries the potential to change unjust practices, but if the women in question are drawn from a narrow elite, if they have been invited rather than elected, and if they have no grassroots constituency to represent and answer to, their presence will be only a token one.

The question, therefore, is to what extent the international community is prepared to provide support to women at the grassroots – support which will ensure that they have the collective capabilities necessary to play this role.

Naila Kabeer is Professorial Fellow at the Institute of Development Studies, University of Sussex. She can be contacted at n.kabeer@ids.ac.uk

Note

1   This article is an edited version of a chapter in *Gender Mainstreaming in Poverty Eradication and the Millennium Development Goals: A Handbook for Policy-makers and Other Stakeholders*, by Naila Kabeer, published by the Commonwealth Secretariat, London, in 2003.

References

Becker, S. (1997) 'Incorporating Women's Empowerment in Studies of Reproductive Health: An Example from Zimbabwe', paper presented at seminar on Female Empowerment and Demographic Processes, University of Lund

Benería, L. and M. Roldán (1987) *The Crossroads of Class and Gender: Industrial Homework Subcontracting, and Household Dynamics in Mexico City*, Chicago: University of Chicago Press

Budlender, D., J. Hicks, and L. Vetten (2002) 'South Africa: expanding into diverse initiatives' in *Gender Budgets Make More Cents*, London: Commonwealth Secretariat

Dolan, C.S. and K. Sorby (2003) *Gender and Employment in High Value Agriculture Industries*, Agriculture and Rural Development Working Paper series, no. 7, Washington DC: World Bank

Goetz, A.-M. (2003) 'Women's political effectiveness – a conceptual framework', in A.-M. Goetz and S. Hassim (eds.) *No Shortcuts to Power: African Women in Politics and Policy Making*, London: Zed Books

Hashemi, S.M., S.R. Schuler, and A.P. Riley (1996) 'Rural credit programs and women's empowerment in Bangladesh', *World Development* 24(4): 635–53

Jejeebhoy, S. (1995) *Women's Education, Autonomy, and Reproductive Behaviour: Experience from Developing Countries*, Oxford: Clarendon Press

Kabeer, N. (1999) 'Resources, agency, achievements: reflections on the measurement of women's empowerment', *Development and Change* 30(3): 435–64

Kabeer, N. (2001) 'Conflicts over credit: re-evaluating the empowerment potential of loans to women in rural Bangladesh', *World Development* 29(1): 63–84

Kabeer, N. (forthcoming) 'From social exclusion to citizenship: wider social impacts of microfinance', in J. Copestake, M. Greeley, N. Kabeer, S. Johnson, and A. Simanowitz (eds.) *Money With A Mission. Microfinance and Poverty Reduction*, Rugby: ITDG Publications

Niranjana, S. (2002) 'Exploring gender inflections within Panchayat Raj institutions. Women's politicisation in Andhra Pradesh' in K. Kapadia (ed.) *The Violence of Development. The Politics of Identity, Gender and Social Inequalities in India*, New Delhi: Kali for Women

Schuler, S.R., S.M. Hashemi, A.P. Riley, and A. Akhter (1996) 'Credit programs, patriarchy and men's violence against women in rural Bangladesh', *Social Science and Medicine* 43(12): 1729–42

Sen P. (1999) 'Enhancing women's choices in responding to domestic violence in Calcutta: a comparison of employment and education', *The European Journal of Development Research* 11(2)

Where to for women's movements and the MDGs?

Carol Barton

This article explores different responses of women's rights activists and organisations, in various regions of the world, to the Millennium Development Goal (MDG) agenda and processes. It gives a brief overview of the current state of play regarding the engagement of women's movements with the MDGs. It then focuses on campaigning and advocacy, and the activism of grassroots movements; women's critiques of the MDGs; and the different ways in which women are choosing to engage with the MDGs, to advance their own agenda.

Women's organisations[1] have had an ambivalent relationship with the MDGs since their inception. When leaders gathered at the UN Millennium Summit in 2000 and agreed on the Millennium Declaration, many women's organisations were engaged in a pitched battle to defend the Cairo Programme of Action (the output of the UN International Conference on Population and Development) and the Beijing Platform for Action (the output of the UN Fourth World Conference on Women) from right-wing assaults, which took place at the five-year reviews of the accords in the same year. Few women's rights activists were focused on the Millennium Summit.

When the MDGs emerged from the UN Secretariat, women's groups were dismayed that gender equality as an issue in its own right was relegated to one quite limited Goal, and that the issue of reproductive rights was not explicit among the Goals. Much more, the Goals appeared to assume a continuation of the Washington Consensus[2] on macro-economic policy, which has increased poverty, particularly for women, and obscured the human rights framework present in the Millennium Declaration. As a result, many women's groups chose to stay on the sidelines.

Over the past two years, however, there have been intense debates among women's groups at the local, regional, and global levels regarding whether to engage, or how to engage, with the MDGs. This reflects a larger assessment of an intense decade of women's organising within the UN arena; the growing strength of the World Trade Organisation (WTO), the International Monetary Fund (IMF), and the World Bank in influencing domestic economic and social policy; the fundamentalist backlash against women's rights; and the relative weakness of women's movements worldwide.

In addition to these concerns, women are debating who sets the agenda of international development and what implications the answer to this question has for advancing their goals, not only of gender equality and women's human rights, but of a just, peaceful and sustainable future for all.

Women's movements at a crossroads

In 2005, women's organisations around the world celebrate a 30-year history of making their voices and demands heard in the UN arena. Since the First World Conference on Women, in Mexico City in 1975, women have used the UN framework to push forward global affirmations of basic rights for women. Nationally, women have then used these commitments to pressure their governments for action. In the decade of the 1990s through to 2001, after the end of the cold war, women used a series of UN conferences to integrate or 'mainstream' gender-equality concerns into such arenas as human rights, population, habitat, social development, the environment, and racism. What emerged from UN intergovernment conferences were plans of action addressing commitments to equality, human rights, peace, and development. In particular, the Beijing Platform for Action, despite the limitations of a consensus document, offered a broad framework for advancing women's equality in 12 critical areas, from the economy, to communications, to health, to peace. In turn, the Cairo Programme put women's reproductive health at the centre of the population and development agenda. The UN World Summit on Social Development (WSSD), held in Copenhagen in 1995, recognised that gender equality is central to the development agenda, that macro-economic policies such as Structural Adjustment Programmes (SAPs) use existing gender inequality to serve their ends, and intensify this inequality as they do so, undermining social development goals. Each of these documents involved commitments, by nations in both the North and the South, to address these concerns domestically and to create an international context that is supportive of these commitments. In addition, each document called on countries to develop plans of action for their implementation.

As women's organisations gained skills in influencing international policy-making and in mobilising for national accountability to commitments, the world was changing around them. The DAWN network (Development Alternatives with Women for a New Era – a 25-year-old Southern-based global feminist network) notes that women's global strategies in the 1990s involved seeking global 'social contracts' through the UN, which could set international standards to be used as tools to put pressure on recalcitrant nation states in relation to issues of women's rights (DAWN 2005).

Yet the WTO, which emerged in 1995, used the same 'supra-national' model to impose a very different agenda, in this case with legal 'teeth'. The WTO served to strengthen the neo-liberal 'free trade' agenda at the expense of a human rights development framework. Increasingly, the notion of policy 'coherence' between the WTO, the IMF, and the World Bank has meant the restructuring of Southern economies and the rewriting of legislation to open national economies further. For many nations, the leverage has been – and continues to be – the massive debt owed to multilateral institutions and private banks, the need for continuing credit, the hope of possible debt relief, and meagre aid.

This poses strategic questions for women's movements. The human rights strategy, while recognising the key role of nation states, has sought to affirm universal rights over national limitations. The WTO strategy succeeded in overriding national sovereignty to undermine those rights, particularly in relation to the formulation of macro-economic policy. Thus, there is a tension between political strategies that defend the ability of nations to set their own economic policy, and strategies that demand a global agenda to respect human rights and environmental and social commitments. This debate will continue as women create responses to this new political moment.

As the global corporate agenda has strengthened its reach, it has increasingly marginalised – or co-opted – the UN as a space for influencing global economic policy, as was evident in the UN Financing for Development process from 2001–2. The UN International Conference on Financing for Development was held in Monterrey, Mexico, in 2002. The Monterrey Consensus represented a deal between the countries of the global North and South, in which poor Southern countries would take more internal responsibility for addressing corruption, adopting fiscal policy perceived as sound by the international financial institutions, and generating internal resources. In exchange, there would be some debt cancellation (with continued conditionalities[3]), opening of Northern markets to Southern goods, and increased Official Development Assistance (ODA).

This deal was incorporated into the MDGs in Goal 8 (global partnership for development). It is worth noting that NGOs, including many women's organisations, rejected the Monterrey Consensus, particularly because it did not address systemic issues of power and wealth distribution in global financial governance.

Despite the consensus, there has been little willingness on the part of the USA and the EU to change their agricultural trade policies or to open markets, as witnessed at the Cancun Ministerial of the WTO in 2003. Similarly, the Heavily Indebted Poor Countries (HIPC) Initiative of the World Bank and the IMF aims to provide meagre debt cancellation in exchange for economic 'reforms', through Poverty Reduction Strategy Papers (PRSPs). In actuality, the PRSP process has led to little debt cancellation. In comparison, it has led to enormous changes in terms of the privatisation of public services, the opening of Southern markets to imports, the end of subsidies for agriculture and other key sectors in poor economies, and the influx of foreign capital and foreign goods at the expense of local economies. As the Gender and Economic Reforms in Africa network has pointed out, this has had a devastating impact on women's livelihoods (GERA 2005).

Alejandro Bendana notes that the notion of 'good governance'[4] and the MDGs have been linked in current development discourse, promoting human rights, democracy, rule of law, property rights, and neo-liberal economics (Bendana 2004). Yet he argues that 'the faulty notion of "good governance" is taking us away from the [MDGs] because it entails placing the state and society at the service of the market' (ibid.). In his view, the Washington Consensus version of 'good governance' is to strengthen the state in terms of its ability to administer economic policies that serve transnational capital. In this equation, governance has been separated from popular democracy and sovereignty. Civil society gets involved as 'stakeholders', not political actors. The IFIs and donors 'limit themselves to procedural definitions of democracy … imposing neo-liberal economic policies as part of liberal political values that … further transfer power towards the top … Both the public and standing governmental structures become disempowered' (ibid.). The global trade and finance regime, and global political misgovernance, are unquestioned in the MDG framework. Hunger and poverty are seen not as political issues, but as technical concerns. Yet, notes Bendana, 'poverty, hunger and bad government cannot be eliminated without the democratisation of policy-making to the most local level possible' (ibid.).

Globalisation and the backlash against women's rights

The world has changed in many other ways too in the time since the UN conferences of the 1990s. Women are experiencing a backlash against equality and human rights, as the outcome of the current rise of the three interrelated forces of economic neo-liberalism, political–religious fundamentalisms, and militarism. While a simple cause-and-effect relationship cannot be implied here, we would argue that the imposition of a hegemonic culture – through markets and media – and the undermining of traditional livelihoods, which are both phenomena produced by neo-liberal economic global-isation, have caused many communities to respond to fundamentalist calls to return to 'tradition'. This is happening in very diverse regions, and among the followers of many religions. While notions of tradition imply a fixed, ahistorical way of being and doing, which may never have existed in the past, the calls to assert tradition have attracted followers set adrift by the cultural and economic uncertainties of the global economy. Many religious fundamentalist groups have also stepped in to provide essential social services to poor communities whom states have abandoned.

Despite their traditionalist stance, the fundamentalists' rise to political power nonetheless builds on and incorporates the corporate global agenda in some instances. In other cases, it utilises an anti-globalisation, anti-imperialist rhetoric that may be appealing to those hurt by the effects of globalisation. One of the key tools in gaining a mass following has been an 'us versus them' mentality. This mentality uses women and the control of their bodies and behaviour as a marker of culture and tradition. 'Our' women are controlled and policed, while 'their' women are attacked, often in brutal ways. This political phenomenon is felt most directly by women in their homes, communities, and countries, but has also been seen at the international level as fundamentalist forces have allied at the UN to push back a women's rights agenda.

Since September 11 2001, the USA has effectively shifted the global debate to 'anti-terrorism' and national security. This has served US internal political interests, while extending US military reach. Development aid is now coupled with deals related to 'anti-terrorism' efforts at home and abroad. As in the USA, copy-cat 'anti-terrorist' policy in countries such as India or Colombia serves to suppress internal dissent (Danner and Young 2003). Meanwhile, as critics including Naomi Klein argue, the overt intervention of the USA and its allies in Iraq seeks to cement US economic dominance in the region (Klein 2003, 2004). Recent and current civil wars in various countries of Africa, including Liberia, the Democratic Republic of the Congo, Sudan, Somalia, and others, are in part the result of the collapse of weak states and national economies, poverty, as well as transnational economic interests (from oil, to diamonds, to natural gas, to private security systems) (Deen 1999; Elbadawi and Sambanis 2000). In the midst of this, thousands of lives are lost and thousands are displaced, poverty has increased, states are further weakened, and violence against women intensifies.

It is in this context that women are asked to engage with the MDGs, which address a development agenda but not the broader context of fundamentalisms, war, foreign intervention, and a main focus on national security.

In the quest for greater government accountability on all women's rights (both personal and economic rights), women's and feminist organisations have been assessing how to reposition their UN advocacy, given the global factors discussed earlier in this section. At the international level, some are also active in advocacy aimed at the IMF, the World Bank and the WTO, the G8, and private industry, and also in anti-war movements.

This global advocacy builds on work at the local and regional levels, around economic rights (such as efforts to secure good-quality jobs, assert land rights, and reclaim public goods), peace (such as national peace-building efforts and post-conflict negotiations), and personal rights (anti-violence, control over women's bodies and choices, reproductive health, sexual rights, and legal protections). Of greatest importance is the need to advocate for these rights in an integrated way that does not prioritise one set of rights while ignoring others, forcing women into impossible trade-offs. Many women's rights activists are concluding that they must work in multiple arenas at multiple levels, without abandoning one arena for another. Beyond strategic questions about how and when to engage with official institutions in the quest for accountability, the larger question is how women can build movements that can challenge the forces of neo-liberalism, political fundamentalisms, and militarisms in a way that affirms gender equality and all human rights.

Limitations of the MDGs

The MDGs emerged from the UN system as an attempt to develop concrete, measurable commitments that would advance the agendas of the UN conferences of the 1990s and the Millennium Declaration. The goal was to provide real momentum for accountability, including follow-through by the North on the Monterrey Consensus.

There is merit in focusing on a few concrete goals and mobilising energy to achieve them after decades of setbacks. Yet there are also serious limitations. Among many critiques that women have raised about the MDGs are the following:

- The MDGs drastically limit the scope of their attention, and set a minimalist agenda.

- They are a technocratic effort to solve systemic political issues, which have to do with global distribution of power and wealth between and within nations.

- In their initial formulation, they have omitted too much of the Beijing and Cairo agendas (as well as the outcomes of other key UN conferences); and they restrict their focus on gender equality,

including it as one of the eight Goals. For example, they include Goals related to HIV, maternal health, and gender equality, but have left out the overall Cairo goal of universal access to sexual and reproductive health care for all by 2015. In so doing, they vastly reduce government accountability on women's rights and obscure key concerns such as violence, labour, reproductive rights, and women's unpaid labour. This is critical: overcoming male domination of women in the private sphere of the household, violence against women, and the invisibility of women's unpaid labour in the economy are all central to women's ability to secure their own livelihoods and participate in development.

- The MDGs do not use the human rights framework of the Millennium Declaration, which includes affirmation of the UN Convention on the Elimination of All Forms of Discrimination Against Women (CEDAW), and the depiction of people as 'rights holders' who can mobilise to demand the realisation of their rights, rather than as 'stakeholders'.

- They seek to eradicate poverty with a top–down approach that virtually excludes poor people, particularly women, from decision making.

- They assume that growth, via macro-economic policies that conform to the Washington Consensus, is the means to eradicate poverty; even when per capita income fell in 54 countries in the 1990s during the years of this same 'economic reform' (Bendana 2004).

- The MDGs focus on implementation in the global South, without mechanisms of accountability being set up to govern the actions of nations of the North. For peoples in the South, this is particularly important in relation to Goal 8 on 'global partnership', which calls on the North to increase aid, support debt reduction, and open markets in the North to Southern goods. For peoples in the North, this is problematic because it apparently absolves their governments of responsibility to address issues of poverty, gender equality, and environmental sustainability within their own borders (commitments that they made in the 1990s).

All this goes some way to explain women's reticence to embrace the Goals, and why Peggy Antrobus, in her article in this issue and elsewhere, has referred to them as 'Major Distraction Gimmicks'.

Yet, as the UN system and bilateral and private donors mobilise their resources to implement the MDGs, and the Beijing ten-year review (Beijing+10) in March 2005 is minimised on the global agenda, many women also feel that they need to be where the action is, to influence and shape policy and the flow of resources. At the local level, many Southern countries are developing plans to implement the MDGs that ignore gender and Beijing commitments. A second Millennium Summit in September 2005 (MDGs+5) will measure progress on the MDGs and may continue to ignore gender issues if women's voices are not present. So the ongoing task is to discern where the key battles are, and how much should be invested in the process.

One further aspect of the debates among women's organisations is about the extent to which donors may be setting the agenda. Many government and private donors have embraced the MDGs, and are seeking civil society partners. Funds are flowing for MDG work. For struggling women's groups and other civil society organisations, it is hard to ignore this reality. This creates further tensions, and many groups have expressed doubts about the process. After many negative reactions to the MDGs in the early stages, some groups are now getting on board because they find that their donors are tying funding to MDG engagement. Others feel they can engage with the MDGs and use

them as a tool to advance their agendas. These issues are part of an important dialogue in which women's organisations are just beginning to engage. The Association for Women's Rights in Development (AWID) is conducting a broad study on the sources and nature of funding for women's movements, and their implications for the kinds of agenda that these movements can consequently further. For women's groups, a key question is how to assess strategically the political impact of engagement in particular issues at this moment, in the context of their own agenda, and grounded in their particular local realities.

Women mobilising for action

Women's organisations have responded in multiple ways over the past two years, often reflecting different regional realities as well as where they find themselves in global social movements and *vis-à-vis* donors. What is beginning to emerge are efforts to use the MDGs to continue to advance women's broader social-justice agenda, without being distracted by the limitations of the MDG conceptual framework.

At the global level, women activists are insisting on the importance of integrating the Beijing+10 and MDG+5 Reviews. This entails demands that commitments made in Beijing in 1995 be reflected in efforts to implement the MDGs, and that these commitments be structured into the debates and official outcome documents of these intergovernment meetings. This work is also being done at a conceptual level by NGOs. As an example, the International Planned Parenthood Federation (IPPF) Western Hemisphere Region and partners hosted two symposia in 2004 to explore the centrality of sexual and reproductive health in relation to the MDGs. Their meeting in Rio de Janeiro in December 2004 addressed the interaction between the MDGs, sexual and reproductive health and human rights, health-sector 'reform', and macro-economic policy in Latin America and the Caribbean (Girard 2004). Similarly, women's groups concerned with poverty have been working to influence the Global Call to Action against Poverty (GCAP – see later in this section) by integrating women's equality as an essential element of poverty eradication. DAWN comments, 'our ability to critically engage with the MDG process is conditioned upon a strong reaffirmation of Vienna, Cairo and Beijing' (ibid.).

The Millennium Project, an effort directed by Jeffrey Sachs, Special Adviser to the UN Secretary-General on the MDGs, aims to refine MDG indicators and provide more specific targets and indicators for implementation (Sachs 2005). This work has drawn on the involvement of task forces for most of the Goals. Women working on these task forces have made intense efforts to introduce gender equality into all of the Goals. Those working on the Task Force on Education and Gender Equality have recommended expanding the targets and indicators to reintroduce elements of the Beijing Platform and Cairo commitments, including women's access to land, women's unpaid labour, violence, reproductive rights, including abortion rights, adolescent sexual education, and labour rights (Grown *et al.* 2005). Significant work was also done in the Task Force on Child Health and Maternal Health and several other task forces of the Millennium Project to incorporate strategies, additional targets, and indicators on sexual and reproductive health. The Sachs report recommends 'protection of sexual and reproductive health and rights (including access to information and family planning services)' (Sachs 2005, 30).

Many women advocates note that the Millennium Declaration is strongly grounded in a human rights perspective and is the intergovernment agreement that frames the MDGs. Others have observed that the MDG Roadmap, issued by the UN Secretariat, recognises that the MDGs do not

supersede Cairo and Beijing commitments (UN 2001). These are important points of leverage in ensuring that this new development initiative remains grounded in international treaties and previous intergovernment commitments.

Other priorities include efforts to integrate national plans of action for Beijing and Cairo with national MDG plans; and a focus on expanding MDG indicators through advocacy at the national level to affect national plans. Another priority is to reaffirm and utilise the human rights framework of the Millennium Declaration. This includes initiatives to use CEDAW as a tool for national accountability on gender-sensitive implementation of the MDGs from a human rights perspective.[5] There are efforts, particularly by women trade unionists, to highlight the creation of good-quality jobs as a necessary part of poverty eradication, the first MDG. This reflects recommendations of the ILO World Commission on the Social Dimension of Globalization (ILO 2004).

A very interesting initiative of civil society groups, supported by the UN Millennium Campaign, is GCAP, launched with the support of President Lula da Silva at the World Social Forum in Brazil, January 2005. The campaign brings together groups working nationally and/or internationally against poverty, and seeks to build global momentum for the MDGs on civil society's own terms. That is, the campaign focuses on what member organisations see as the bottom-line steps for progress on the MDGs, including fair terms of trade, debt cancellation, an increase in quality and quantity of aid, the creation of anti-poverty programmes that are accountable to citizens, and the attainment of gender equality.

REPEM, a Latin American feminist network, and DAWN, an international network, have been involved in the co-ordination of the campaign. Other feminist groups have joined the process, seeking to strengthen gender perspectives in the campaign. They organised a high-profile launch of the campaign during the Beijing+10 Review in New York in March 2005.[6] GCAP is open to interested organisations, and is primarily nationally based, building on ongoing anti-poverty work and global economic-justice programmes. This campaign will hold a White Band Day on 1 July 2005 at the time of the G8 meetings, and will be present at the World Bank and IMF Meetings (April), the Millennium Summit (September), and the WTO Ministerial (December) (GCAP 2005). As noted above, feminists are working to make their voices heard in this process.

Regional responses

Africa

There seems to be a higher level of engagement on the part of women with the MDGs in Africa, where a large number of governments are working with the IMF and the World Bank within the PRSP framework, and are particularly dependent on promised foreign aid and possible debt reduction. One of the problems here is how to reconcile PRSPs, which have often entailed cuts in government services, with the MDGs to eradicate poverty, infant and maternal mortality, and infectious diseases.

Women's groups see the MDGs as an entry point to try to reclaim the right to public services that dramatically affect their lives, and to point out the contradictions with the PRSP process. A new initiative, the African Women's Millennium Initiative for Fighting Poverty Through Gender Equality (AWOMI) seeks to do just this. The Director, Yassin Fall, notes that because Goal 3 on gender equality is central to all of the other Goals, 'the MDGs propose concrete steps that women can use as initial actions towards realisation of Beijing recommendations' (AWOMI 2005). She notes that women's involvement has been relatively marginal to the PRSP processes, and women's movements have been ill-prepared to shape MDG plans nationally. Thus, AWOMI seeks to define

monitoring mechanisms and instruments for implementing MDGs through the leadership of women, and to train women to participate. AWOMI wants to ensure that any resources mobilised for the MDGs are put in the hands of poor women leaders at the local level. Likewise, Hellen Wangusa of the Millennium Campaign sees the MDGs as a critical entry point for African women to engage with their governments in a critique of the PRSP process, and to strengthen the hand of local officials *vis-à-vis* the IFIs. It is an opportunity to push for an end to privatisation of water supplies, health care, education, and other basic services, to seek national control over economic policy-making, and to insist on debt cancellation as a necessary step towards achieving the MDGs.

Latin America

The issue of reproductive rights, ignored in the MDGs, has been central to the feminist agenda in Latin America. Consequently, some Latin American feminist groups have wanted little to do with the MDGs. A gathering of Latin American feminists at the 2005 World Social Forum in Porto Alegre was entitled, 'We Don't Want a Few Goals, We Want All of the Platform!'. However, others are exploring how to imprint their agenda on the MDG framework. Susanna Chavez of Flora Tristan, a 25-year-old Peruvian feminist organisation, notes:

in the current climate of conservatism and fundamentalisms, the MDGs do not encompass the full historic accumulation and recognition of human rights. The MDGs are minimal in order to set a global baseline, but as such, they do not oblige mid-sized semi-industrialized countries to advance further. Thus, the MDGs may actually limit human rights demands and aspirations since they set lower standards than Cairo and Beijing and governments may perceive them as sufficient to meet their commitments.
(Allen and Falu 2004, 41)

The response of Flora Tristan has been to promote additional indicators nationally, which raise the bar. As noted earlier, the conference in Rio de Janeiro in 2004, sponsored by the IPPF Western Hemisphere Region, gathered regional feminists to explore how to affirm reproductive rights within the MDGs. Several events at the 2005 World Social Forum, including one co-sponsored by the Latin American and Caribbean Committee for the Defence of Women's Rights (CLADEM), sought to '"engender" the MDGs'.[7]

Asia

Responses to the MDGs in Asia reflect a reality of poverty, racial, ethnic and caste divisions, and militarism. Women's responses have often been linked to those of broader social movements with which they work. The statement of the Asian Civil Society Forum, held in Bangkok in November 2004 by the Conference of NGOs (CONGO), and including women's and feminist organisations, affirmed 'critical engagement' with the MDGs. They focused on the Millennium Declaration, which underscores the need for a human rights perspective for the implementation of the MDGs, and also affirmed the UN Declaration on the Right to Development:

the MDGs can be meaningfully achieved only if issues of exclusion and discrimination, as well as structural causes of poverty ... are made central to the implementation process ... Governments and relevant agencies have to draw on international commitments and obligations [to gender equality] as set out in ... the Beijing Platform ... and ... CEDAW.
(Asian Civil Society Forum 2004)

The Asian Civil Society Forum expressed concerns about the potential use of the MDGs to justify privatisation of public services, proposals emerging from the Millennium Project to promote genetically modified organisms, and the perception of marginalised sectors as 'stakeholders' instead of rights-holders. The members called for commitments from the North on Goal 8, including debt relief, fair trade, and aid, and for a reduction in military spending to meet MDGs and their 'related livelihood rights' (ibid.). The groups made a concrete suggestion of using the MDGs as 'one of the tools that enable the advancement of human rights and sustainable development within the context of people's ongoing struggle for their basic right to live and sustainable livelihoods' (ibid.). They called for alternative people-centred reports on MDG implem-entation, participation in the MDG+5 Review, and in the 5th WTO Ministerial in Hong Kong in December 2005. Sunila Abeyesekera of the Sri Lankan human rights organisation, INFORM, who was present at the event, described the rationale as follows:

as women's rights activists, we are faced with the challenge of engaging in a serious attempt to transform the MDGs at the national level, to fulfil at least some of our most primary aspirations in terms of women's health and education, while at the same time engaging in a critical evaluation of the overall implications of reducing the sum total of human aspirations in the 21st century to a few basic needs ... In particular, the framework for fulfillment of the MDGs [must] confront and overcome violence and discrimination against women and guarantee the equality of women within the family and in the 'private sphere'.
(Abeyesekera 2004, 7)

Europe

Some women's organisations in Europe, particularly the Nordic countries, have taken on the task of holding their governments accountable on Goal 7 (environment) and Goal 8 (global partnership), while continuing work to convince both govern-ments and NGO colleagues to integrate gender analysis and a commitment to gender equality into these Goals. KULU (Women in Development of Denmark) is one such group engaged in this process.

Conclusion

As we have seen, many women are reluctant players in the MDG game, but they continue to feel the need to be at the table to push for a gender-equality agenda that is integrated into all areas of development and peace. They are not conceding any terrain on Beijing and Cairo commitments, but many are using the MDGs as a vehicle to keep women's issues on the global agenda. They are challenged to link with other social movements, and to address systemic macro-economic issues, while insisting on the need for gender justice and an integrated analysis of inequality, including race/ethnicity, caste, and class. This means strengthening women's movements and organising to tackle the powers behind neo-liberalism, fundament-alisms, and militarism. It means, also, being strategically present in multiple international arenas, from the UN, to the G8, to the WTO, while strengthening local work. It is always a dual task to convince male allies that the feminist agenda is central to the social-justice agenda and to mobilise with these allies to challenge entrenched power. Despite global backlash, there are signs of vitality in women's movements, including young women organising around feminist concerns, and the Feminist Dialogues (2005). These, among others, offer hopeful signs for the future.

Carol Barton is co-ordinator of Women's International Coalition for Economic Justice (WICEJ) (www.wicej.org), a coalition of more than 40 organisations from all regions of the world, addressing gender and macro-economic policy from an integrated feminist perspective which explores gender, race, and class oppressions.

Notes

1 I differentiate here between women's organisations and feminist organisations. Women's organisations may organise around women's needs, including a social and economic agenda, but may not claim to be feminist. I refer to feminist organisations, self-defined, as groups that bring a systemic analysis of patriarchy to their activism. I refer to women's movements (plural) because they are many and diverse.

2 The Washington Consensus refers to a set of policy prescriptions emanating from the IMF and the World Bank which have encouraged the opening of markets, a reduced role for the state in the economy, and export-oriented growth.

3 'Conditionalities' here refers to the economic and legal prescriptions urged by the World Bank, the IMF, Regional Development Banks, and often bilateral donors, as a condition for aid, credit, or debt relief. Early on, these included calls to liberalise trade, focus on exports, cut wages and social spending, and devalue currency. More recently, conditions have included calls to privatise public goods and enterprises, and to change laws and even constitutions to comply with WTO rules and guarantee the rights of foreign capital.

4 As understood within the UN and international financial institution (IFI) development context, 'good governance' refers to national government commitments to adopt 'responsible fiscal policy', contain corruption, and establish legal structures that enable capital, particularly foreign capital, to be managed according to predictable rules. It does not tend to refer to respect for human rights, including economic and social rights, people's political participation, equitable taxation, national economic sovereignty, or other concerns of civil society.

5 The United Nations Development Fund for Women has a new resource to assist women's organisations in this area; see UNIFEM (2004).

6 Co-sponsors included, among others, ActionAid, AWID, Centre for Women's Global Leadership (CWGL), Comité de América Latina Y el Caribe Para la Defensa de los Derechos de la Mujer (Latin American and Caribbean Committee for the Defence of Women's Rights – CLADEM), INFORM Sri Lanka, International Confederation of Free Trade Unions (ICFTU), International Gender and Trade Network (IGTN), International Women's Health Coalition (IWHC), Red de Educación Popular Entre

Mujeres, Sancharika Samuha (Women's Media
Forum) Nepal, Women's Environment and
Development Organization (WEDO), and
Women's International Coalition for Economic
Justice (WICEJ).

7 The CLADEM event was called 'Reviewing the
MDGs with a Gender Lens'. It was co-sponsored
with other partners, including Social Watch.

References

Abeyesekera, S. (2004) 'Development and women's
human rights', in C. Barton and L. Prendergast
(eds.) *Seeking Accountability on Women's Human
Rights: Women Debate the UN Millennium
Development Goals*, Mumbai: WICEJ,
www.wicej.addr.com/mdg/index.html

Allen, A. and A. Falu (2004) 'Engendering the
MDGs in the Andean region', in C. Barton and
L. Prendergast (eds.) *Seeking Accountability on
Women's Human Rights:Women Debate the UN
Millennium Development Goals*, Mumbai: WICEJ,
www.wicej.addr.com/mdg/index.html

Asian Civil Society Forum (2004) 'Statement on
Millennium Development Goals', www.acsf.info
(checked February 2005)

AWOMI (2005) 'African Women's Millennium
Initiative for Fighting Poverty through Gender
Equality', AWOMI (unpublished concept paper)

Bendana, A. (2004) ' "Good Governance" and the
MDGs: Contradictory or Complementary?',
paper presented at the Institute for Global
Network, Information and Studies conference,
Oslo, 20 September 2004. Published in *Focus on
Trade* 105, Focus on the Global South,
www.focusweb.org

Danner, M. and G. Young (2003) 'Free markets and
state control: a feminist challenge to Davos Man
and Big Brother', *Gender and Development* 11(1):
82–90

DAWN (2005) 'Remaking the Social Contract',
DAWN Supplement for the World Social Forum,
Porto Alegre, Brazil, 26–31 January 2005

Deen, T. (1999) 'Diamonds Cause of African Civil
Wars', Media Institute of Southern Africa/Inter
Press Service, 17 March 1999

Elbadawi, I. and N. Sambanis (2000) 'Why are there
so many civil wars in Africa? Understanding
and preventing violent conflict', *Journal of
African Economies* 9: 244–69

Feminist Dialogues (2005)
http://feministdialogue.isiswomen.org/
(checked February 2005)

GCAP (2005) www.whiteband.org (checked
February 2005)

GERA (2005) http://twnafrica.org/gera/
gera_default.asp (last checked February 2005)

Girard, F. (2004) 'The Millennium Development
Goals and Sexual and Reproductive Health in
Latin American and the Caribbean', summary of
symposia discussions, International Planned
Parenthood Federation Western Hemisphere
Region (www.ippfwhr.org), Rio de Janeiro, 30
November 2004

Grown, C., G. Rao Gupta, and A. Kee (2005) 'Taking
Action: Achieving Gender Equality and
Empowering Women', Millennium Project Task
Force on Education and Gender Equality,
Earthscan, London,
http://unmp.forumone.com/
eng_task_force/GenderEbook.pdf (checked
February 2005)

ILO (2004), 'A Fair Globalization: Creating
Opportunities for All', www-ilo-
mirror.cornell.edu/public/english/wcsdg

Klein, N. (2003) 'Privatisation in disguise', *The
Nation*, New York, 15 April 2003

Klein, N. (2004) 'Outsmarting terrorism with
outsourcing', *The Nation*, New York, 6 March
2004

Sachs, J. (ed.) (2005) 'Investing in Development – A
Practical Plan to Achieve the Millennium
Development Goals',
http://unmp.forumone.com/ (checked
February 2005)

UN (2001) 'Roadmap Towards the Implementation
of the UN Millennium Declaration', Secretary-
General's report, UN, 6 September 2001,
A/56/326, www.un.org

UNIFEM (2004), 'CEDAW, Beijing and
the MDGs Resource Guide',
www.mdgender.net/resources/

Approaches to reducing maternal mortality:

Oxfam and the MDGs

Arabella Fraser

The political momentum of the Millennium Development Goals (MDGs), coupled with a technical consensus about how to tackle maternal mortality, greatly improves the prospect of reducing women's death and disability rates. In its campaigning and advocacy work on the MDGs, Oxfam will focus on the need to raise the national and international finance for the investments that this requires. Finance is a necessary, but not sufficient, condition for change to the lives of millions of women who suffer as a result of pregnancy and childbirth – and it is sorely lacking. This is no argument for technical quick-fixes, however. International efforts to reduce maternal mortality must concentrate on improving health systems – a project that entails rebuilding states to deliver services – but they must also look to an advocacy grounded in women's rights, as articulated in the Beijing Platform for Action and the Cairo process.

Oxfam and the MDGs

Oxfam has adopted the MDGs as a framework for action in 2005 and beyond, in the belief that they represent an unprecedented opportunity to combat global poverty and suffering. The commitments made by developed and developing-country governments in 2000, the constellation of events in 2005 (in particular the UN Special Assembly on MDG progress), and the political momentum that this is now generating provide civil society organisations with a critical opportunity to effect change. Undoubtedly, the aims of the MDGs fall far short of the eradication of global poverty and suffering: it is estimated that reaching the Goal 1 target to halve income poverty would still leave 694m people living on less than $1 a day in 2015 (Pogge 2003); but it is also true that they should be both realistic and achievable. They represent a mechanism for political accountability that is linked to outcomes and is multi-sectoral – delivering results where it matters, to tackle the broad underlying causes of poverty. The sad fact is that, despite all this, the MDGs are under threat. Only the target of halving income poverty has any chance of being met, and even this is due to progress in just a few countries (World Bank and IMF 2004). Suggestions are even emerging to the effect that the MDG deadlines should be postponed to 2050 (Painter 2004).

The importance of the MDG on maternal health

The high level of maternal death in the developing world is a tragedy in itself. It reflects a gross violation of human rights by the world's governments. At a conservative estimate, at least 530,000 women die each year from causes related to pregnancy and childbirth (WHO, UNICEF and UNFPA 2003) – a toll that amounts to one death every minute. On top of this, severe pregnancy-related complications induce high levels of morbidity, affecting around 15 million women each year and in many cases leading to long-term disability. The impact on family and community is equally stark. Beyond the immediate suffering and grief caused, maternal deaths diminish children's own life chances. Death rates for these children, measured over the two years after their mothers' deaths, are between three and ten times higher than for children with both parents living (Panos Institute 2002). Recent estimates for Africa, where almost half of all maternal deaths take place, are that between 2001 and 2010 there will be 2.5m maternal deaths, 7.5m child deaths, and 49m maternal disabilities, with a cost to economic productivity of US$45m (WHO 2004).

More than any other indicator for health, maternal mortality figures reveal huge gulfs between rich and poor countries. The risk of death over the course of a woman's reproductive lifetime in the UK is 1 in 3,800; the figure is 1 in 8,700 in Canada (WHO, UNICEF and UNFPA 2003). But in developing countries, the risk is of a different magnitude. In Sierra Leone and Afghanistan, a woman's lifetime risk of maternal death is 1 in 6. Estimated maternal mortality ratios,[1] the basis for the MDG target, are 13 deaths per 100,000 live births in the UK, compared with 1,800 in Malawi. Maternal mortality-related measures also show the depth of national disparities in access to health care. In Yemen, half of all women in the richest quintile are cared for by a skilled attendant at birth, compared with less than 10 per cent for the poorest women (Public World 2004).

The outlook for progress on maternal mortality is currently grim. On current trends, only 17 per cent of developing countries are likely to meet the target of reducing the maternal mortality ratio by three-quarters (Wagstaff and Claeson 2004). Maternal mortality ratios have barely declined in many developing countries, and have even increased in Africa, exacerbated by the spread of HIV / AIDS (DFID 2004).

The MDG on maternal health, for which maternal mortality is the specific indicator, is also significant within the theoretical context of gender and the MDGs. Out of seven outcome-based targets, only two – on gender equity and education, and maternal health – are specifically directed at issues of gender inequity. As Lynn Freedman has argued previously in *Gender and Development* in response to criticisms of the limited attention paid to gender in the MDG framework, 'there is space for feminist action around the remaining MDG on reducing maternal mortality' (Freedman 2003). It is the only goal with an explicit connection to women's health, but it also represents an opportunity to highlight the political, cultural, and economic barriers that women face when seeking access to health care.

A new opportunity for progress

Setting international targets to reduce maternal mortality is not new. In 1987, the Safe Motherhood Conference set the objective of reducing the number of maternal deaths by at least half within a decade. However, the conditions for action on maternal mortality have changed, meaning that the MDG set of targets should be operationalised more effectively. First, there is far greater knowledge about maternal health than ever before. The first global estimates of maternal mortality were not made until the mid-1980s (Standing 2004). Measuring maternal mortality is still difficult: under-reporting, incorrect diagnosis, and poor recording systems make statistics unreliable, and the measure of deliveries by skilled health personnel is commonly used as a proxy for maternal mortality ratios. Nevertheless, since the founding of the Safe Motherhood Initiative in 1987, a vast body of evidence has been generated about its causes and consequences (Weil and Fernandez 1999).

There is also a much clearer consensus than at any time previously about the strategies required to reduce maternal mortality. Based on the fact that 80 per cent of all deaths are caused by complications (in particular haemorrhage, or severe bleeding, infection, hypertensive disorders, and obstructed labour) that are easily treatable, it is recognised that the interventions with greatest life-saving potential are (1) the provision of skilled attendants at birth and (2) Emergency Obstetric Care, with an effective referral system in place to ensure that when complications are identified, women access the necessary health care (Freedman *et al.* 2004). In the 1980s and early 1990s, practitioners focused on training Traditional Birth Attendants (TBAs) and providing antenatal care. Both are important aspects of improving attendant factors to maternal mortality, such as poor nutrition or anaemia, which increase a woman's susceptibility to complications. However, neither alone will bring down death rates. Complications are difficult to predict, meaning that antenatal care is unlikely to be able to identify women at greater risk. And when potentially fatal complications do occur, attendants need to possess a far higher level of skill than can be expected of TBAs. Even then women may ultimately require access to emergency care facilities capable of performing Caesarean section operations and blood transfusions. There has also been increasing recognition that although family planning reduces the number of pregnancies, and therefore the number of deaths, it does not alter the risk of dying once pregnant (Weil and Fernandez 1999).

Both developments are the result of a broader shift in attitudes to maternal health, away from seeing it as instrumental to population control and child welfare, to recognising it as an end in itself (Kabeer 1994). This is an important step. In a study of the preconditions for reducing maternal mortality in industrialised countries, De Brouwere, Tonglet, and Van Lerberghe identify the following as key factors: awareness of the magnitude of the problem, a recognition that it is avoidable, and the mobilisation of health professionals and the community (De Brouwere *et al.* 1998). There

are certainly more grounds than ever before to believe that these preconditions are coalescing at an international level for a reduction of maternal mortality in the developing world.

Financing gains in maternal mortality

One of the main obstacles to capitalising on these trends is the failure to finance maternal health. Increased finance alone is not a sufficient condition for achieving progress, but it is nevertheless a necessary one. In the absence of additional finance for countries with high maternal mortality levels, the MDG will undoubtedly be missed.

Developing-country governments need to allocate greater shares of their public budget to basic social services. In Abuja in 2001, African governments committed themselves to devote at least 15 per cent of their spending to improving health services; but almost all countries in sub-Saharan Africa allocate less than 10 per cent of their budgets for this purpose (Oxfam International 2004). However, for developing countries to mobilise the necessary resources to improve health services will take many years – and women are dying today. The Commission on Macroeconomics and Health estimates the additional cost of providing an essential health 'package' in low-income countries at more than double current average health budgets. Even allocating developing-country expenditure more efficiently, the amount that developing countries could mobilise by 2007 would be less than half the level required to cover a basic health package, with a 30 per cent shortfall in 2015 (Commission on Macroeconomics and Health 2001). For the poorest countries, marginalised from the global economy, aid is the only source of finance that can be released in the time-frame and in the predictable, targeted manner required to fill the financial gap to meet the MDGs. It is for this reason that the MDGs include a requirement for rich countries to provide more generous aid.

The scale of mortality rates can create the impression that resolving the problem will require vast financial resources. However, the investment needed is relatively modest. The World Bank and World Health Organization (WHO) estimate that the cost of providing basic maternal services averages around US$3 per person in developing countries (Goodburn and Campbell 2001). The total cost of such health coverage for sub-Saharan Africa would amount to around US$1.5bn. This is just half a day's total health spending in the USA. The annual incremental cost of cutting maternal mortality by 75 per cent is around US$4bn – a price equivalent to 0.01 per cent of the combined GDP of the OECD countries, or just two days' worth of military spending by the G8 countries.

Yet the major aid donors have yet to make available the necessary finance. Overall, at least US$50bn extra a year is estimated to be necessary to meet the MDGs, and the value of existing aid is reduced by such practices as tying aid to the purchase of goods and services in the donor countries (Oxfam International 2004). Countries continue to pay out more in debt service than they spend on essential health services: 10 out of 14 African countries included in the Heavily Indebted Poor Country (HIPC) Initiative, which aims to relieve countries of heavy debt burdens, continue to spend more on debt repayments than health (ibid.). Meanwhile, major health initiatives remain starved of cash: at the 1994 Conference on Population and Development, developed countries agreed to pay around one-third of the cost of a programme to deliver sexual and reproductive health and rights to all by 2015. Despite a target of providing US$5.7bn by 2000, only US$2bn of this amount was made available (UNFPA 2003). Aid to the health sector in general has been increasing, in large part due to concerns about the

HIV/AIDS epidemic, but it remains low: in 2002, aid to health and population programmes amounted to only 8 per cent of development assistance (DAC 2004). Of this, it is difficult to tell how much is allocated to programmes that contribute to reducing maternal mortality (a problem in itself), but just over one-third supports reproductive health-care and population activities, one-third funds basic health care, while the rest goes to general health care and non-basic health services. Studies from 1990 showed finance for reproductive health to be strongly biased towards family-planning programmes; 42 per cent went to family planning, while just 0.2 per cent went to Safe Motherhood programmes – the main initiative at the time with responsibility for maternal mortality (Standing 2004).

Financing health-care services that are responsive to women's needs

Maternal mortality ratios highlight the importance of investment in building effective health systems. Indeed, maternal mortality rates are often seen as a key indicator of the state of a country's health system, with poorly functioning systems unable to supply the necessary skilled personnel and emergency obstetric facilities. More broadly, the effect of the MDGs has been 'to place the expansion and improvement of basic public services at the heart of international development policy' (Public World 2004). The UN Task Force on Child Health and Maternal Health describes weak health systems as 'the primary obstacle to meeting the MDGs' (Freedman *et al.* 2004).

Without doubt, legal, managerial, and human-resource reforms need to accompany the provision of finance for health systems. However, it also needs to be recognised that the potential for institutional and organisational change is undermined by the lack of resources. In addition, undertaking to build effective health systems has implications for the type of international finance provided. Donors will need to finance recurrent costs, salaries, and maintenance, not just one-off capital investments. Funding needs to be predictable and long-term. Donors need to move away from funding their own stand-alone projects and other vertical programmes. Oxfam's own research in Ethiopia reveals that current HIV/AIDS programmes could divert around half of existing health personnel away from their current activities (Fraser 2004).

The capacity of states in the developing world to provide such services is weak, and has been weakened further by Structural Adjustment Policies. Many governments reduced health expenditure in real terms in the 1980s and 1990s: Zambia's per capita spend on health fell by 50 per cent each decade, for example (Public World 2004). It is estimated that Africa will require 1m additional health workers to ensure the staffing required to deliver basic health interventions (High-Level Forum on the Health MDGs 2004). Health care is now provided by a plethora of actors – not just the private sector, but NGOs and faith-based organisations as well as traditional healers. However, for Oxfam, investing in state provision is vital, as the state is theoretically the only provider with the means to ensure nationwide, equitable, and sustainable coverage. As Oxfam set out in 2000, leaving such social provision to the market leads to inequity in access and reinforces income inequality, with the poorest people having to put aside a greater proportion of their incomes to pay for services, which in the health sector are often highly unpredictable and large (Watt 2000). Introducing market mechanisms into state structures has a similar effect: in Yemen the introduction of user fees meant that one person in two could not afford basic health treatment, thus either forgoing the treatment or accumulating debts to pay for it (Public World 2004). Particularly pertinent for reducing maternal mortality rates is the fact that decisions about

paying for services may not be taken by women themselves, and where cost places increased constraints on families' use of health care, women's health needs are not prioritised.

An important lesson from the history of universal state provision is that equity is not guaranteed. Studies in the UK show that although the introduction of universal free health care in the late 1940s led to dramatic reductions in maternal mortality, there was little impact on inequality between income groups (Watt 2000). There is little current work focused on how to ensure gender-equitable state health provision, although a key component of this is known to be the quality of care, with studies showing that the interpersonal skills and attitude of staff are as important an influence on women's decisions to seek care as are their technical skills (Buttiens et al. 2004). In Yemen, female patients identified the lack of a female medical practitioner as an important reason for not using state health-care services (Public World 2004).

Engaging with rights-based approaches to reducing maternal mortality

As a rights-based organisation engaged in monitoring the MDGs, Oxfam has a keen interest in forging links with the constituency of analysis and practice that emerged from the Cairo process and the Beijing conference in the 1990s. What the International Conference on Population and Development in Cairo in 1994 did was to link sexual and reproductive health to rights for the first time, emphasising women's empowerment and the provision of universal, high-quality reproductive health services (Standing 2004). These commitments to gender equality and reproductive health were reinforced at the Fourth World Conference on Women, or the Beijing Platform for Action (ibid.). Elements of the constituencies that fought so hard to achieve this in the 1990s are critical of the MDG process, on the following basis: it represents no more than a 'Most Distracting Gimmick', which diverts attention from international agreements made prior to the MDGs – agreements that have greater potential to advance women's equity and empowerment (Antrobus 2004); and the absence of a rights-based framework means that the MDG indicators are devoid of important notions of agency and empowerment and pay insufficient attention to vulnerable groups (Robinson 2004) as well as the power relations that affect women, which sanction among other things violence both in the family and the community (Abeyesekera 2004).

Engagement with this powerful critique is vital for all working on the MDGs, but in particular for those concerned with maternal mortality. Indeed, authors such as Hilary Standing partly attribute the slow progress on improving reproductive health services to insufficient dialogue between the protagonists of reproductive health (associated with Cairo) and health-sector reform (increasingly associated with the MDGs). Yet, first, attention to a human rights framework leads us to understand that although the emergence of a 'technical consensus' is a major breakthrough, there is no technical quick-fix. For the supply of modern health care to be effective, there also has to be demand. Among poorer women, although the need for care will be greater, the ability to access care may be limited by their status, as women are not economically or socially able to take their own decisions about seeking health treatment. In parts of Afghanistan, for instance, women are not permitted to leave home unless accompanied by a male family member (Oxfam GB 2004). Uneducated women are less likely to recognise complications when they occur, although there is no established relationship between education and using health-care facilities. In addition, the relationship is often context-specific, and countries such as

Bahrain and Kuwait have reduced levels of maternal mortality, despite women's low status (McCarthy and Maine 1992).

Second, attention to a human rights framework draws attention to the fact that sexual and reproductive rights, agreed upon at the International Conference on Population and Development in Cairo in 1994, were deliberately written out of the MDGs by a US-led conservative alliance. This has ramifications for donor and government policies relating to women's reproductive choices, with a knock-on effect on maternal mortality. The most striking example of this is US policy on abortion. The Bush administration in 2001 restored the 'Mexico City Policy', which prohibits funding for groups that provide or promote abortion. With 18 per cent of all maternal deaths attributed to unsafe abortion, it is of grave concern that the largest bilateral funder of health programmes in the world is not tackling this issue – and despite the evidence that abortion continues even when better family planning is available (Pearson and Sweetman 1994). The rule has also meant cuts to health programmes around the world, with funding to the United Nations Fund for Population Activities (UNFPA), the largest multilateral source of assistance for reproductive health and population pro-grammes, stopped for three years in a row, while Population Action International has charted the closure of clinics in Bangladesh, Ghana, and Kenya and cuts to reproductive health services in Tanzania and Ethiopia as a result (*Observer* 2004).

A rights-based perspective also reveals the underlying socio-economic and cultural causes of women's poor health. Socio-economic and cultural factors indirectly increase the risks of maternal death. Women with less education are likely to have more pregnancies earlier and are more susceptible to HIV/AIDS and other sexually transmitted diseases. Cultural pressures may mean that women bear children at a younger age, with pregnancy the leading cause of death among women aged 15–19 years worldwide. Violence against women compounds health problems during pregnancy: a study in Bangladesh confirmed that 14 per cent of maternal deaths were due to violence (UNICEF 2003). However, the links between these underlying causes and actual death rates are difficult to prove precisely, and it is now clear that action on these causes by itself will not reduce maternal mortality ratios. Tackling them is, however, not only important in its own right, but certainly affects maternal health more broadly – and the stated aim of Goal 5. And both reducing maternal mortality and improving maternal health are affected by the political and legal status of women, which governs effective supply of relevant health care and circumscribes the legal rights of women, with particular reference to laws relating to the legal age for marriage, and laws relating to rape and female genital mutilation.

Conclusion

The planned events of 2005 are a huge opportunity to push governments to deliver on their commitments to the MDGs. Success would mean the release of vital resources to rebuild health systems to provide universal, equitable, and high-quality coverage in countries with high maternal mortality rates. In addition to this, welcome practical suggestions are emerging to stimulate debate on how to bring the Cairo and Beijing frameworks to bear upon the MDGs – ensuring that due attention is paid to sexual and reproductive rights and women's empowerment. This involves influencing national planning around the MDGs. It means looking to the Millennium Declaration, not just the narrow indicators of the MDGs, which includes commitments to 'combat all forms of violence against women and to implement the Convention on the Elimination of All Forms of Discrimination Against Women (CEDAW)'. And it means taking advantage of the fact that the ten-year

review of the Beijing conference will occur in the same year as the five-year review of the MDGs, to exploit the synergies between the two.

This article is adapted by Arabella Fraser from The Cost of Childbirth, *written by Arabella Fraser, Dr Mohga Kamal-Smith, and Kevin Watkins (Oxfam GB 2004). Arabella Fraser is a researcher at Oxfam GB on MDGs and international finance, and the author of* Paying the Price, *Oxfam International's latest report on financing for the MDGs (Oxfam International 2005).*

Note

1 Maternal mortality ratios, used as the indicator for the MDG, measure the number of maternal deaths per 100,000 live births. This is different from maternal mortality rates, which reflect the number of maternal deaths per 100,000 women aged 15–49 and capture not only the risk of death but also the number of pregnancies per year.

References

Abeyesekera, S. (2004) 'Development and women's human rights', in C. Barton and L. Prendergast (eds.) *Seeking Accountability on Women's Human Rights: Women Debate the MDGs*, New York: Women's International Coalition for Economic Justice

Antrobus, P. (2004) 'MDGs – the Most Distracting Gimmick', in C. Barton and L. Prendergast (eds.) *Seeking Accountability on Women's Human Rights: Women Debate the MDGs*, New York: Women's International Coalition for Economic Justice

Buttiens, H., B. Marchal, and V. De Brouwere (2004) 'Skilled attendance at childbirth: let us go beyond the rhetoric', *Journal of Tropical Medicine and International Health* 9(6): 653

Commission on Macroeconomics and Health (2001) *Macroeconomics and Health: Investing in Health for Economic Development*, Geneva: WHO.

DAC (2004) *Development Cooperation 2003 Report*, Paris: OECD

De Brouwere, V., R. Tonglet, and W. Van Lerberghe (1998) 'Strategies for reducing maternal mortality in developing countries: what can we learn from the history of the industrialised West?', *Journal of Tropical Medicine and International Health* 3: 771–82

DFID (2004) 'Reducing Maternal Deaths: Evidence and Action', London: DFID

Fraser, A. (2004) 'Financing the MDGs in Ethiopia', Oxford: Oxfam GB (unpublished)

Freedman, L. (2003) 'Strategic advocacy and maternal mortality: moving targets and the millennium development goals', *Gender and Development* 11(1): 97–108

Freedman, L., M. Wirth, R. Waldman, M. Chowdhury, and A. Rosenfield (2004) 'Millennium Project Task Force 4: Child Health and Maternal Health', www.unmillenniumproject.org/documents/tf4i nterim.pdf (last checked by author December 2004)

Goodburn, E. and O. Campbell (2001) 'Reducing maternal mortality in the developing World', *British Medical Journal* 322: 917–20

High-Level Forum on the Health MDGs (2004) 'Addressing Africa's Health Workforce Crisis: An Avenue for Action', www.hlfhealthmdgs.org/ Documents/AfricasWorkforce-Final.pdf (last checked by author December 2004)

Kabeer, N. (1994) 'Implementing the right to choose', in N. Kabeer *Reversed Realities: Gender Hierarchies in Development Thought*, London: Verso

McCarthy, J. and D. Maine (1992) 'A framework for analyzing the determinants of maternal mortality', *Studies in Family Planning* 23(1): 23–33

Observer (2004) 'Dying to have a baby', 11 October 2004 (www.mariestopes.org.uk/ pdf/dying-to-have-a-baby.pdf)

Oxfam GB (2004) *The Cost of Childbirth: How Women Are Paying the Price for Broken Promises on Aid*, Oxford: Oxfam GB

Oxfam International (2005`) *Paying the Price: Why Rich Countries Must Invest Now in a War on Poverty*, Oxford: Oxfam International

Painter, G. (2004) 'Gender, the Millennium Development Goals and Human Rights in the Context of the 2005 Review Processes', Gender and Development Network (draft)

Panos Institute (2002) *Birth Rights: New Approaches to Safe Motherhood*, London: Panos Institute

Pearson, R. and C. Sweetman (1994) 'Abortion, reproductive rights and maternal mortality', *Focus on Gender* 2(2): 45–50

Pogge, T. (2003) 'The First UN Millennium Development Goal', paper presented at the University of Oslo, 11 September 2003

Public World (2004) 'Delivering Good Quality Public Services: Health and Education', Oxford: Oxfam GB (unpublished)

Robinson, M. (2004) 'Mobilising people to claim rights', in C. Barton and L. Prendergast (eds.) *Seeking Accountability on Women's Human Rights: Women Debate the MDGs*, New York: Women's International Coalition for Economic Justice

Standing, H. (2004) 'Towards reproductive health for all?', in R. Black and H. White (eds.) *Targeting Development: Critical Perspectives on the Millennium Development Goals*, New York: Routledge

UNFPA (2003) *Achieving the MDGs: Population and Reproductive Health as Critical Determinants*, New York: UNFPA

UNICEF (2003) 'A Human Rights-Based Approach to Programmes for Maternal Mortality Reduction in a South Asian Context', Kathmandu: UNICEF

Wagstaff, A. and M. Claeson (2004) *The Millennium Development Goals for Health: Rising to the Challenges*, Washington DC: World Bank

Watt, P. (2000) *Social Investment and Economic Growth: A Strategy to Eradicate Poverty*, Oxford: Oxfam GB

Weil, O. and H. Fernandez (1999) 'Is safe motherhood an orphan initiative?', *The Lancet* 354: 940–3

WHO (2004) 'Fourth International Meeting on Women and Health', www.who.or.jp/ women/publications/0310_p.pdf

WHO, UNICEF, and UNFPA (2003) 'Maternal Mortality in 2000', http://millenniumindicators.un.org/unsd/mi/ mi_source_xrxx.asp?source_code=51 (last checked by author December 2004)

World Bank and IMF (2004) 'Global Monitoring Report 2004 – Policies and Actions for Achieving the MDGs and Related Outcomes', http://siteresources.worldbank.org/GLOBALM ONITORINGEXT/Resources/DC2004-0006-Add1(E)-GMR.pdf

The education MDGs:

achieving gender equality through curriculum and pedagogy change

Sheila Aikman, Elaine Unterhalter, and Chloe Challender

This article argues that there is a need for gender-sensitive curricula and pedagogies in schools in order to achieve good-quality outcomes for girls' education. It examines different dimensions of gender equality and draws on issues raised and discussed at two international seminars which challenged narrow views of curriculum and pedagogy. The article considers these issues in the context of a case study of the abuse of school girls in Mozambique, and NGO and community strategies to combat such abuse. It presents important actions that need to be taken by governments, teacher-training organisations, and NGOs to ensure that change occurs.

Today, millions of girls who attend school are the first in their families ever to do so. Yet for many of them, gender inequality is not only a feature of the political, economic, and social conditions in which they live, but often pervades their educational experience.

At the Millennium Summit of the UN, Millennium Development Goal (MDG) 3 was broadly framed to 'promote gender equality and empower women'. Within the Goal, the target relating to education was set in terms of eliminating gender disparity in primary and secondary education prefer-ably by 2005 and in all levels by 2015 (www.un.org/millenniumgoals).

Eliminating gender disparity is generally taken to mean overcoming barriers to equal access to, and sometimes achievement in, schooling for girls and boys. Gender parity can be measured simply in terms of whether or not there are equal numbers of girls and boys in a population enrolled in school or completing school (UNESCO 2003).

The disjuncture between the wide framing of the Goal and the narrow focus of the target on education has prompted considerable discussion and debate (Millennium Project 2004). Recent e-discussions have broadened the focus from gender parity to gender equity and quality of education.[1] These include the uneven quality of education provided, the high levels of dropout, and the difficulties that many girls (the majority, in some societies) have in progressing beyond a few years of formal schooling. In other words, those working to achieve Education For All need to look beyond access to schooling and examine what happens within the school. Moreover, unless urgent attention is paid to addressing inequalities of gender (and race and ethnicity) that shape girls' experience of education in classrooms around the world, the narrower project for increasing access to education may also be undermined.

The 'Beyond Access: Gender, Education and Development' Project, launched in April 2003, aims to disseminate knowledge and support policy and practice changes that will achieve gender-equitable education and meet the 2005 MDG 3 on eliminating gender disparity in primary and secondary education.[2] It has engaged policy makers, researchers, and practitioners through seminars and discussions to identify strategies for achieving gender equality in formal education. This article draws on the papers and discussion from two international seminars: 'Curriculum for Gender Equality and Quality Basic Education', September 2003, in London, and 'Pedagogical Strategies for Gender Equality', February 2004, Nairobi (see www.ungei.org and Aikman and Unterhalter 2004). These seminars examined the impediments to achieving a gender-sensitive, quality education that will provide benefits for learners. This article focuses on schooling and examines practices of curriculum and pedagogy which promote a quality education for girls and boys. Through a case study from northern Mozambique, the article considers one community's attempts to ensure gender justice for girls and changes in the practice of education in school. The article ends by suggesting important actions that need to be taken by governments, teachers training institutions, NGOs, teachers, and communities to ensure that these changes occur.

Curriculum and pedagogy for gender equality

In this section, the article examines two important issues beyond access: the need to ensure curricula that promote gender equality and gender-equitable pedagogical practices. By emphasising pedagogy as 'the teacher–learner relationships involved in child-rearing as well as in schooling' (Weiner 2000), we recognise that definitions of pedagogies are contested and that there are different approaches to what is good pedagogy and what promotes learning.

Gender equality should be integral to ideas of educational quality, since gender equality entails the removal of deep-seated barriers to equality of opportunity and outcome, such as discriminatory laws, customs, practices, and institutional processes. It also entails concern with the development of the freedoms of all individuals, irrespective of gender, to choose

outcomes they have reason to value. The existence of gender equality in the classroom is therefore important in connecting schooling with citizenship, based on a vision of equal rights. An education system should develop the full capabilities of children, through offering an education that is personally and socially worthwhile. Children need the freedom to enter school, to learn and participate there in safety and security, to develop identities that tolerate others, to promote health, and to enjoy economic, political, and cultural opportunities.

Gender issues and the curriculum

The curriculum is a key piece of national legislation. There are important questions to be asked regarding what girls are being taught about themselves in formal schooling, whether education institutions allow girls effective participation, and whether the existing situations of girls and women are enhanced or diminished by the schooling they receive. The kind of education that girls and women want is shaped by their experience and expectations of what they can do with education in the future. The expectations of girls and their parents regarding the curriculum that they study may be formed through social, economic, or political constraints in the immediate environment or deduced from development rhetoric about the benefits schooling brings for individuals and society.

While a range of declarations and conventions provide written support for ideas about gender equality and human rights, the ways in which these values can form a part of the process of putting a curriculum into practice have been hardly considered. This is an important area for governments, NGOs, and community-based organisations to consider. There is not a single model demonstrating how this might be done, but Box 1 outlines some recommendations.

The *who* and the *what* of curriculum are not confined to the content, but also to the processes of curriculum development and the forms of consultation and debate that

Box 1: Rights, gender equality, and questions about curriculum

---

Rights and participation: *Who* (which groups) are defining what is to be taught and how it is to be delivered? (To what extent are women a part of this?)

Rights and conceptions of the person: *What* are girls being taught about who they are in their education?

Rights and institutions: *Do* the processes in which education is institutionalised and delivered allow girls' effective participation? Are girls'/women's existing situations enhanced or diminished through the education they receive?

Yates (2004)

---

underpin the choice of ideas, documents, and materials that comprise a curriculum and its process of review. Given extensive gender inequality worldwide, but also widespread commitment to challenge and overcome it, improving decision making about curriculum policy and gender equality is an important challenge.

Women and girls possess other identities that create differences between them. Hence, care needs to be taken that a broad range of views of women and girls from different social groups are included in curriculum development and review processes. The presence of women in decision-making bodies at national and local government levels, for example in South Africa (see Chisholm 2004), has had an extremely beneficial effect on shaping a curriculum that is responsive to diverse needs.

Sometimes girls' and women's expectations of what schooling should offer them are hampered by their limited knowledge of social policies. When involving women and girls in decision making, it is necessary to provide insights that go beyond the immediate and familiar context so that decision making is well informed. Formal schooling must not be at the expense of the knowledge and the skills that girls and women have of their local context, but being responsive to these particularities needs to go together with an education which helps girls to realise their freedoms and selfhoods and participate fully in forms of society that they value.

Pedagogies

Teachers are central to the delivery of the curriculum. How do teachers, who possess different social identities and are themselves located within gendered social relations, translate curriculum documents into classroom practices and learning outcomes? And how do these practices influence further curriculum development, particularly with regard to gender equality?

Decisions about what teaching methodologies, learning materials, teacher training, and resources to use are dependent not only on what is available but also on what is considered appropriate by those who make decisions about developing and defining pedagogical approaches. Different pedagogies imply different social dynamics of a classroom, including not only relations between teacher and learner but relations between different groups of learners and dynamics between teachers and officials and others such as parents and the local community. These relations are often marked by social divisions – of race, class, ethnicity, and gender. Boys and girls need to participate in learning as equals. Pedagogies that fail to achieve this render the goal of equal access meaningless.

But side by side with these relations of difference are pedagogies that express aspirations for relations of equality. Teachers and learners construct approaches to gender, race, class, ethnicity, and sexuality in different ways at different times. This means that social relations and ideas about gender and other social divisions are open to change. Maintaining gender inequalities in a classroom, for example, is not a 'natural' process: it entails deciding not to change.

Problems with girls' learning are diverse: for example, teachers commonly have low expectations of the intellectual abilities of girls, and girls have correspondingly low expectations of themselves. These low expectations are reinforced by textbooks and curriculum and examination materials. Teachers often say that they enjoy teaching boys more than girls, especially if girls are seen as passive. They may also offer a lower level of feedback to girls. There is a widespread lack of female teachers in high-status subjects, and an overall lack of female teachers. Finally, the use of physical space in school playing fields or classrooms can marginalise girls (Arnot 2004).

Across the world, schooling has not always fulfilled its potential as a change agent capable of challenging existing gender inequalities. Assumptions about what is appropriate for boys and girls to learn often undermine aspirations for equality in pedagogy. For example, in many societies, it is assumed that girls cannot learn mathematics, and that boys cannot learn about the care of young children. As discussed in the section on curricula, historical and geographical contexts play a crucial role in shaping these assumptions, and creating the conditions in which an agenda for gender equality does or does not develop. Curriculum divisions and the pedagogies that accompany them may entrench gender inequalities. For example, if only boys practise public speaking or play the sports that are linked with national prestige (football or cricket for example) and girls are excluded from these activities but encouraged to concentrate on learning domestic skills, inequalities regarding how young people express citizenship are entrenched.

At a general level (clearly it will differ according to contextual factors) we might expect to see a pedagogy that promotes gender equality to include the following:

- changes to the curriculum and to classroom organisation that allow for increased participation of girls and women (and other under-represented groups of students);

- encouragement of critical questions about the curriculum and what counts as school knowledge;

- a breaking down of hierarchies and power-networks that exclude girls and women, whether they are students or teachers;

- greater understanding of the conditions that lead to bullying, racism, sexism, and homophobic behaviour, and more successful forms of intervention;

- greater valuing of students' experience and knowledge, and closer involvement of students in planning and evaluating their educational work (Weiner 2004).

This pedagogy might be expected to result in an increased consciousness among students of misconceptions, prejudices, and stereotypes, and the ability to criticise and challenge these. It would also result in a stronger sense of agency in all involved in learning, which would enable them to visualise wider and more varied options in life (ibid.).

Appropriate pedagogy involves living as well as teaching gender equality. There is considerable evidence from many different settings across continents of classroom practice that is far from acceptable, and widespread instances of sexual harassment and violence at school. The majority of accounts point to teachers and male pupils as being involved in sexual harassment of female teachers and primarily girl pupils. The issues touch on how teachers not only teach gender equality, but how they *live* this in areas of their life that are considered private. Studies in seven African countries show how the relationship between male teachers and girl students is often constructed as sexualised (see Chege 2004).

Thus pedagogy for gender equality is not only a matter of professional orientation, but also of changing personal behaviour among teachers and other education officials, and challenging some of the deeply held assumptions that perpetuate inequalities.

Case study: addressing sexual abuse of girl pupils in northern Mozambique

This section draws on an example from northern Mozambique to show the actions that can be taken by an NGO and community to begin to overcome sexual abuse of girls in school, which is one of the worst manifestations of gender inequality.

Oxfam GB has been working in the province of Zambezia on a programme aimed at capacity building for basic education, with a strong focus on gender equality, since 2000.[3] It work with the Mozambican Association for Gender and Education (AMME), providing capacity building and supporting AMME to develop its ways of working at the community level. Together with Oxfam, AMME has lobbied the Ministry of Education for legislation concerning abuse of girls in school. In 2003, they achieved a landmark ruling by the Ministry of Education against a teacher in Zambezia province. This work was carried out by AMME and the Committee Against the Abuse of Girls in the community of Lioma, Gurue District.[4] AMME has been supporting women teachers and gender training for community members, School Councils, and teachers in Zambezia province. In addition, it has been encouraging community-based organisations to tackle gender inequalities and abuse in their communities and schools.

In 2003, in the village of Lioma, sexual abuse of a school girl came to light when the girl herself came forward and denounced a teacher who had made her pregnant. It was subsequently found that he had abused several girls. AMME supported the villagers to take the case to the local Tribunal. In the absence of formal procedures by the Ministry of Education, the District Education Department was slow to respond and did nothing and later suggested a transfer of this teacher to another school. So AMME took the case to the Provincial Department of Education, which eventually acted: the teacher was suspended and subsequently dismissed. As a result of lobbying by AMME and other organisations, a new Ministerial Decree was passed, which now provides clear steps for District and Provincial Ministries to take in cases of abuse in school. AMME's work has brought this new legislation to the attention of teachers, who now realise that they cannot act with impunity. AMME reports that, because of this awareness, sexual abuse of students by teachers appears to be declining; however, it is still prevalent in the wider society, particularly by traders.

After the abusive teacher had been held to account, other girls in Lioma began to come forward to report incidences of abuse. Concern in the community was so strong that it created a Committee Against the Abuse of Girls. Fortified by the capacity building and support that the School Council has received from AMME and Oxfam, the new Committee set up a Counselling Centre in the village to help victims of abuse in schools and in the community. With some training from AMME and a little money to repair an old house, the Centre is now open on two evenings a week for anyone to drop in. Between January and June 2004, 18 cases of abuse of girls and young women were reported to the Committee, including abuse by teachers and fellow students. These cases are being taken to the local Tribunal. The Committee now has plans to expand its awareness-raising about the problem of abuse to localities nearby.

Capacity building and support for new forms of community organisation, such as School Councils and the Counselling Centre, are enabling community members to play an active part in promoting gender equality and gender justice in their own schools and villages. Women and girls are becoming members of both the Council and the Committee, though they are still in a minority. But they have broken their silences, and their voices are beginning to be being heard in the school and the wider community in Lioma. The Lioma case is not unique – both in terms of the abuses and inequalities faced by girls and women, and in the initiatives taken to turn the tide.

Teachers and training for gender-sensitive curricula and pedagogy

The Mozambique case study provides an example of the widespread harassment of girls by male teachers – ranging from verbal and physical abuse to sexual abuse – that is a major influence on girls' decisions to drop out of school. Girls and female teachers are often assigned chores such as fetching water, cleaning classrooms, and cooking for the (male) head teacher. Teachers may use these tasks as a pretext for luring girls into their houses, where they are sexually abused (Muito 2004). The HIV/AIDS epidemic gives an added urgency to the need to deal with this unacceptable dimension of school life. In challenging inequalities or abusive relationships, particularly in the era of HIV/AIDS, it has become clear that teachers themselves have to learn how to guide their students' sexuality and provide living examples of low-risk behaviour.

It is essential to support and train teachers to promote gender equality. Even in contexts in which there are extensive gender inequalities outside school, teachers *can* make a difference inside school. They can work with a diversity of girls' and boys' learning styles so that all children's styles can be accommodated in the class. When teachers, teacher educators, and school managers work together to develop classroom strategies incorporating a diversity of styles, then all students can excel.

Attempts to make schools more 'girl-friendly' involve challenging the ethos of authority, hierarchy, and social control that pervades the majority of schools, and developing ways of engaging with rights, empowerment, agency, and the voice of the learner. Where school management is gender-responsive, gender-equality strategies are developed not only for administrative issues, but also for management of the curriculum, the personal and social development of students, and the participation of students in decision-making (see Box 2). Through School Management Committees and School Councils, the possibility now exists in many countries for greater decision-making and influence by learners and community members in schools, on issues that include gender.

Box 2: Tuseme *clubs*

The Forum for African Women Educationalists (FAWE) took teachers at a small number of schools in Kenya, Rwanda, Senegal, and Tanzania through a *tuseme* ('speak out') programme, with good results for girls and boys. In *tuseme* clubs girls learned how to analyse their educational problems and find ways of solving them.

Teachers and school managers also attended *tuseme* workshops, as well as having training in guidance and counselling. This encouraged them to work with the students to create stimulating and gender-sensitive learning environments that were not restricted to the academic aspect of their work but encompassed the social ethos of the school.
Mlama (2004)

Teachers and school management need to be aware of how their pedagogies and the curriculum can sustain gender inequalities and have severe consequences for girls' and boys' learning. 'Gender sensitisation' is not enough to empower teachers to develop gender-responsive teaching methodologies and pedagogies that go beyond recognising gender stereotypes and questioning stereotypical expectations of boys and girls. Gender differences pervade the choice of learning style, assessment, students' ability to express their voice and use space, as well as how reforms geared to developing 'independent learners' are expressed and implemented.

Very little work has been done in teacher-training courses to develop teachers' understanding of gender inequalities and how to overcome them in the classroom. To address the issues of both teachers' professional and personal orientation, opportunities are needed for student teachers and teachers in-service – who may have had only very limited pre-service training, or none at all – to understand their own gender socialisation and identities, and to understand how gender discrimination takes place in schools, as well as their role in addressing it (Chege 2004). Because the issues are complex, a single training session, either at the pre-service stage or through in-service, is generally not sufficient to change teaching practice and behaviour. And any training that does not extend to supporting teachers to develop practicable solutions and is not accompanied by monitoring and follow-up support will have limited impact. Where training *is* co-ordinated and effective, it is not well documented, with the result that knowledge of strategies and learning is not captured and utilised. So, strategies need to be explored for storing the knowledge about gender-equitable pedagogies that is developed at schools and training centres, in order that teachers and teacher trainers can benefit from lessons already learned and experience already gained.

Teachers face multiple problems and challenges in their personal and professional lives, including low pay and poor conditions, which contribute to low morale and low status. To return to the Mozambique example, AMME has been carrying out a range of initiatives since 2000, which aim to build the cultural, social, and economic knowledge of women teachers. It has also attempted to address some of the problems faced by primary-school teachers. These include very low standards of living for all teachers. Female teachers' status and opportunities boomed briefly during the socialist regime in Mozambique in the 1980s, but the ensuing civil war undermined previous gains, and female teachers today are struggling for equal access to benefits, resources, and opportunities for promotion. The situation is slowly changing as women teachers begin to demand greater participation in decision-making within schools and within the education system. There are now examples of women school directors and school cluster directors,[5] although they are still a small minority. Other changes taking place that can reinforce the principle of equal rights and opportunities for women in the teaching profession include the establishment of Gender Units in District Departments of Education, although these suffer from a chronic shortage of funding and resources.

Women teachers and directors are providing positive examples of what women can achieve, in the rural areas of Zambezia. AMME, Oxfam, and the District Department of Education are working together with a multi-faceted approach to improving access, retention, and quality outcomes for girls in primary schooling. This has included building houses for female teachers, supporting the District Gender Unit to develop its terms of reference and planning, offering bursaries to girls from some of the most economically disadvantaged households, and investing in girls' hostels so that they can easily access upper primary school.

As AMME testifies for the rural Mozambique context, female teachers often struggle against abuse from male colleagues and students, while at the same time being expected to be active transformers of the system, to assess textbooks, audit the curriculum, develop the local curriculum, and develop new classroom practice. Expectations of teachers to become effective change agents for gender equality – inside reformers – will not be met unless teachers are supported and empowered to do this through the co-ordinated efforts of pre-service training institutions, and providers of in-service and ongoing professional development. Local contexts are very important in defining the nature of support needed and the nature of gender inequalities, such as unequal power relations, gender-based violence and HIV/AIDS, poverty, and employment (C Lege 2004).

What can be done, and to what do we aspire?

There are three broad scenarios for the coming ten years with regard to our aspirations for the MDGs and therefore with regard to what is achieved. In the first scenario – a 'business as usual' approach – we continue with the current patchy implementation of policies and programmes for gender equality, concentrating primarily on improving access and leaving the responsibility for pedagogies to small units within education ministries, a handful of NGOs, and certain concerned teachers and education officials. Larger numbers of children will come into school, but only some will learn in ways that help them to thrive. A considerable number will be subject to threat and violence in school. Strategies to combat sexual abuse of girls in school, such as in Lioma, will continue; but funding and support may remain unreliable and short term, provided through NGOs and community-based organisations with little institutional support or follow-up.

In the second scenario – realising the Dakar Framework – we will have achieved Education for All, as laid out in the Dakar Programme for Action, and all children will be in school. But the ways in which improved education quality and enhanced pedagogies link with gender equality will have been only partially fulfilled, because of a focus on the formal education system to the exclusion of wider societal considerations. The Lioma school will nevertheless be supported by good implementation of the current curriculum reform in Mozambique, by improved school/community relations through the School Council, and by enhanced training for teachers in gender equality and increased numbers of female teachers.

In the third scenario – gender-equal pedagogies for enhancement and confidence, inclusion and participation (Arnot 2004) – the full vision for gender equality as laid out in the Beijing Platform for Action, the resolutions taken at other key international forums such as Cairo in 1994 (International Conference on Population and Development), and the World Summit on Social Development in 1995 will have been realised. This means that gender-equitable pedagogies will be based in broader societal change for gender equality, with implications for the sustainability of practice. In Lioma, girls will no longer be preyed upon by traders and others in the community, because they will be empowered to demand that their rights are respected and their positions in society are strengthened. They will benefit from an education which provides them with the capabilities to achieve the freedoms they want and the kind of lives they value. Table 1 illustrates the potential of each scenario.

The opportunities provided by the global push for the MDGs will have been lost if in 15 years' time we have only achieved Scenario 1. To move towards Scenarios 2 and 3, this article has highlighted a range of strategies which, as part of a coherent and integrated approach, will help to achieve gender equality in education. These are drawn

Table 1: Scenarios for pedagogy and gender equality

Aspects of the school experience and environment	Scenario 1: Business as usual	Scenario 2: Realising the Dakar Framework	Scenario 3: Pedagogies for enhancement, inclusion, and participation
Entering school	Partially achieved	Achieved for all	Achieved for all
Retention in school	Only some stay in school	Achieved for all	Achieved for all
Learning successfully	Only some learn	Some do not learn	Achieved for all
Developing tolerant identities	Receives little attention in school	Only some develop tolerant identities	Achieved for all
Experiencing safety and security	Safety and security is very fragile	Only some experience safety and security in school	Achieved for all
Promoting health	Very little promotion and experience of health	Some do not experience this	Achieved for all
Facilitating economic, political, and cultural opportunities and outcomes	Achieved for some children	Increasing numbers achieve this	Achieved for all

together below in terms of the types of action that need to be taken by different actors.

Policy makers and government officials

It is crucial that policy makers and government officials promote institutions that are fair to women and men and promote gender equity as a fundamental value. Such institutions will provide an environment for furthering dialogue between policy makers and practitioners where both are alert to the insights of the other with regard to gender-equality strategies. This will help to ensure that there is a questioning of the current gendered ways in which decisions about curriculum content and curriculum development are taken, and that measures are instigated to ensure that they do not reinforce inequalities. The policy-development process needs to involve not only government officials and donor experts but teachers, teacher trainers, students, parents, and the wider community. Listening to girls and parents about their expectations is vital for the design of realistic and good policies.

School heads and teachers

Policies need to be translated into practical curricular and pedagogical responses which challenge gender inequalities and pay particular attention to eradicating abusive or violent relations. Head teachers need to provide good leadership with support from local education authorities and communities so that the ethos of the classroom and school is 'girl-friendly' and the female teachers feel supported and safe. Within classrooms, teachers can involve pupils by asking them how they learn best and by attending to the voices of all, particularly those who are least often heard. Here, teachers' skills in participatory methodologies and responding to different learning styles are important. They can involve students in developing strategies for gender equality through a process of change regarding pedagogies and the curriculum. Teachers can work with students, developing what they already know, and can directly challenge both their own and students' use of offensive stereotypes by making explicit rules about gender equality with regard to class participation, rather than relying on informal understandings.

The teacher trainers

Governments have a major responsibility for helping to develop gender equality in pedagogy through the courses that they provide for teachers. Many NGOs and government-supported institutions also provide teacher-training courses. Training is needed that helps to develop teachers' understandings of gender-equality issues and how to overcome them in the classroom. This will involve training of the trainers too. There is a need for teacher-training modules that concentrate on gender equality and provide packages of practical materials for teachers to use in classrooms. Training packages need to be suited to local contexts, but materials already exist that can be sensitively adapted.[6] For teachers to be able to change pedagogies and overcome the taken-for-granted gender inequalities that are part of the societies in which they live, they need on-going support. One way of creating this support may be through building networks of teachers to work together on new pedagogies through school clusters and teachers' centres. Sustaining training and learning for teachers and education officials will be enhanced by building networks and through sustained support to implement ideas about gender equality and pedagogy. Action research networks focusing on gender equality are a useful way forward, as are networks that link girls together.

Schools and teachers working with communities and parents

Teachers, NGOs, and community-based organisations need to work closely with parents and communities to develop ways to support girls' and boys' learning so that they can all participate in the life of their communities. Parents' anxieties or misgivings about schooling for their daughters need to be taken seriously, but the opportunities for educated daughters and

sons on completion of at least a basic education also need to be illustrated to stimulate aspirations, as do role models. This article has provided one example of how community leaders and elders have been part of a process of awareness-building around gender equity and schooling, which has met with considerable success.

Sufficient resources

Resources are vital for the above initiatives and strategies to be implemented. Time is an important resource, which is key to the development of a coherent and integrated approach. But training and capacity-building are also essential, as well as the funding to allow these other resources to be realised.

Good documentation and communication

An integrated and coherent approach depends on access to good information and documentation about what has worked and what has not worked in different contexts and conditions. It is also dependent on building new networks of communication, and the exchange of learning and experience for on-going policy development and improved practice. These networks need to make new links between entrenched channels of communications, such as within ministry hierarchies or NGO–partner relationships, to allow for new and challenging forms of engagement and interaction between groups.

Conclusion

This article has shown that gender equity for girls in education is much more than a matter of equal access. It has considered practices which militate against girls' retention and achievement in school – sexual abuse, in the Mozambican case – and illustrated how factors and influences both inside and outside the school contribute to persistence of extreme gender injustice. Improving the quality of girls' and boys' education means investing more resources,

54

commitment, and sustained support for teacher education and curriculum change. Achieving gender equality in education for the enhancement, inclusion, and participation of all girls means that educational quality must be accompanied by broader changes in society. For the girls of Lioma, the MDGs must deliver change to allow them to achieve the freedoms to which they have a right, and the kind of life that they value.

Sheila Aikman is the Global Education Policy Adviser with Oxfam GB and co-ordinator of the DFID-funded 'Beyond Access: Gender, Education and Development' Project. She has worked and published on intercultural education, indigenous education, and gender, with a special focus on Latin America. Email: saikman@oxfam.org.uk

Chloe Challender writes and edits materials for the 'Gender, Education and Development: Beyond Access' project. She facilitates the flow of information concerning the project to a wide audience around the world, organising conferences, seminars, and events linked to the project. Email: c.challender@ioe.ac.uk

Elaine Unterhalter is Senior Lecturer in Education and International Development at the Institute of Education, University of London. She co-ordinates the 'Gender, Development and Education: Beyond Access' project. Email: e.unterhalter@ioe.ac.uk

Notes

1 For example, the right2education e-discussion for civil society feedback on the Millennium Project Task Force's interim report on achieving the MDG on gender equality, co-ordinated by ActionAid, the Commonwealth Education Fund, and the Global Campaign for Education, June 2004 (www.unmillenniumproject.org/html/tf3docs.shtm).

2 The project is co-ordinated by Dr Elaine Unterhalter and Dr Sheila Aikman with Chloe Challender and Rajee Rajagopalan. A joint project between the Institute of Education, University of London, and Oxfam GB, it is located at the Institute of Education.

3 Thanks are due for the information in this case study to colleagues in the Oxfam GB Zambezia programme, Ruth Bechtel and Olga Muthambe. The case study is also available in the May 2005 issue of *Links* on the MDGs, which is available online at www.oxfam.org.uk/what_we_do/issues/gender/links/index.htm.

4 Thanks to Maria Isabel Ligonha and Fatima Luciano Muha from AMME for information for this case study, gathered through a semi-structured interview on 24 September 2004.

5 An example from Mozambique is Naipa School in Gile District, Zambezia province, where the female school head is also the director of the local cluster of schools. The impact of providing housing and support for a female head teacher in this remote school has been a 200 per cent increase in girls' attendance (Oxfam GB project note, 7 July 2004).

6 The Beyond Access website contains information about easily available resources: www.girlseducation.org.

References

The following references are to papers prepared for Seminars 1 and 2 of the Beyond Access Project. The materials cited can be found on the Beyond Access website: www.ungei.org or http://ioewebserver.ioe.ac.uk/ioe/cms.

Aikman, S. and E. Unterhalter (2004) 'Curriculum and Pedagogy for Gender Equality and Quality Basic Education in Schools', paper based on the Beyond Access Project Seminars 1 and 2 and presented at the World Congress of

Comparative Education Societies Congress, Havana, November 2004

Arnot, M. (2004) 'Gender Equality and Opportunities in the Classroom: Thinking about Citizenship, Pedagogy and the Rights of Children' (University of Cambridge, UK)

Chege, F. (2004) 'Teachers' Gendered Lives, HIV/AIDS and Pedagogy' (Kenyatta University, Kenya)

Chisholm, L. (2004) 'The Politics of Implementing Policy Gender Equality: Evaluating Gender Equality and Curriculum – The Politics of Curriculum 2005 in South Africa'

Mlama, P. (2004) 'FAWE's Experience in Africa in Changing Teaching for Gender Equity' (Executive Director, FAWE, Kenya)

Muito, M. (2004) 'Gender Equality in the Classroom: Reflections on Practice' (Organising Secretary, FAWE Kenya Executive Committee)

Weiner, G. (2004) 'Learning from Feminism: Education, Pedagogy and Practice' (University of Umea, Sweden)

Yates, L. (2004) 'Does Curriculum Matter?' (University of Technology, Sydney, Australia)

Other references

Millenium Project (2004) 'Achieving Universal Primary Education by 2015', Background Paper of the Task Force on Education, www.unmillenniumproject.org/html/tf3docs.sh tm

UNESCO (2003) *Gender and Education for All: The Leap to Equality*, Paris: UNESCO

Weiner, G. (2000) Book review in *British Educational Research Journal* 28(6): 904–7

Not a sufficient condition:

the limited relevance of the gender MDG to women's progress

Robert Johnson

Despite recent awareness of the need to 'mainstream' gender perspectives into public policy, and in responses to economic inequity and growing poverty, practice often seems to continue to place gender equity as a secondary goal. Are the Millennium Development Goals any different? This article argues that – taking Belize as a case in point – the absence of gender disparities in schooling (the core of the single gender-based Millennium Development Target) has led to neither improved gender equity in the workforce, nor improved gender shares of national income. Even if the gender-relevant Target and associated Indicators are met, the accompanying Goal to 'promote gender equality and empower women' may therefore fall far short of achieving any real progress. Gender equality in education may be a necessary condition for improving gender equity in political and economic relations, but it is not a sufficient condition for doing so.

The new century opened with an unprecedented declaration of solidarity and determination to rid the world of poverty.
(UNDP 2003, 1)

So begins the UNDP *Human Development Report* (HDR) for 2003, subtitled *Millennium Development Goals: a compact among nations to end human poverty*. It is not clear what is 'unprecedented' about such a declaration, in the wake of failed commitments to 0.7 per cent GDP official development assistance by developed states, the poverty-reduction undertakings of the 1995 World Summit on Social Development, the actual effects on poor people of structural adjustment programmes, the International Monetary Fund's (IMF's) Poverty Reduction and Growth Facility, the World Bank's Poverty Reduction Strategy Plan, and other global declarations and initiatives concerning poverty. Perhaps it is that this concerns the *eradication* rather than merely the *reduction* of poverty, which seems a cruel hoax on the world's poor people in the wake of such multilateral failures. If it hasn't been possible to reduce poverty under earlier commitments, what confidence should there

be in the hope of 'ridding' the world of poverty by 2015? The HDR simply observes that 'the 1990s saw unprecedented stagnation and deterioration' in this regard (ibid. 40); and this for the decade that promised the world's poor the benefits of the 'peace dividend' following the end of the cold war.

In his analysis of the feasibility of the poverty reduction objectives of the MDGs, Gaiha concludes that they are overly optimistic, if not misleading. However, he argues, they 'are nevertheless useful in drawing attention to pervasive deprivation in the developing world, and to the need for a determined and co-ordinated effort on the part of the development community to reduce [poverty] substantially in the near future' (2003, 76). Is that the best that can be expected from the MDGs? Who needs such a reminder to try harder? Poor people don't. The developing countries – with increasing external interventions allegedly in their own interests – don't. And those multilateral agencies that pull the levers that have imposed poverty-exacerbating state economic policy are unlikely to change their behaviour due to the MDGs (and neither are they required to do so by the associated performance indicators).

Poverty and inequality, gender and power

Within the dominant framework of poverty reduction and economic growth, lessons have been learned slowly and with difficulty. Neo-liberal policy prescriptions have served to weaken developing-country economies, increase the numbers in poverty, and diminish the interventionist capacity of their governments (in the interests of free markets). Dagdeviren *et al.* conclude that 'growth alone is a rather blunt instrument for poverty reduction, since the consensus of empirical work suggests that typically it is distribution neutral' (2002, 405). Their analysis demonstrates the primary role of redistributive measures – even to the exclusion of a growth scenario – in tackling poverty.

But the interventions of the IMF and World Bank have explicitly served to weaken the capacity of states to perform such roles. Their imposed neo-liberal prescriptions have been additionally counter-productive because they 'widen the global inequality that poverty reduction strategies seek to mitigate' (Nederveen Pieterse 2002, 1042). Those developing countries that survived the economic downturn of the past decade 'were those which refused to listen to the IMF' (Monbiot 2003, 148).

There have been two concurrent trends in recent decades: the parallel increases in global inequality and in global economic integration, and the parallel increases in extreme poverty and wealth. While at a national level inequality is not as politically sensitive a theme as is poverty, at a global level it is the other way around, because poverty can be posited as a fact of life – while inequality concerns power relations:

In that global inequality maps relative deprivation, it challenges the legitimacy of world order in a way that mere poverty statistics, accompanied by benevolent policy declarations, do not ... [B]y prioritising poverty over inequality, relations of power, and the responsibilities these entail, are eliminated from the picture.
(Nederveen Pieterse 2002, 1027)

Of course, at a national level, inequality – insofar as it concerns a gender dimension – can become politically sensitive precisely for that reason: it challenges dominant power relations. It is useful here to draw a distinction between 'condition' and 'position', the former referring to a person's material state (such as levels of wealth/poverty, education, employment/unemployment, vulnerability to violence/abuse), the latter referring to a person's social, political, or economic place in society (Economic Commission for Latin America and the Caribbean 1997, 3). Much of the attention to the situation of women has been addressed to their poorer *condition*: inequitable access to resources and greater need for certain services. This rarely threatens power relations. It is when measures are advocated to address the inferior *position* of women, especially with respect to their equal rights to economic and political power, that systemic resistance is encountered.

Consequently, it has been possible – even normal – to improve the condition of women without hurting the condition of men or challenging the position of men. However, resistance occurs when there is action to achieve greater equity in the position of women, because it is more likely to mean changes in the position of men. Arguably, this has been a central theme of the 'gender and development' agenda. The 'feminisation of poverty' at a national level has been understood as an issue of inequality that extends to the very basis of women's position: in economic relations, in access to power and decision-making, and in the domestic sphere. It is emphatically not addressed in a sustainable manner solely by measures to improve the material conditions of women.

The inclusion in HDRs of gender indicators has helped to focus the treatment of gender within the human development framework. This necessarily involves a consideration of issues of power within states, if not between them or beyond them. A gender perspective has thus been a productive – and essential – means by which the direct relationship between poverty and inequality may be better understood at the national and sub-national levels. For the HDR gender indicators – the Gender-related Development Index (GDI) and the Gender Empowerment Measure (GEM) – the focus is both on gender disparities in the components of the Human Development Index (HDI) (life expectancy, education participation, literacy, and income) and on gender shares of economic and political power (parliamentary seats, positions as legislators, senior officials and managers, positions held as professional and technical workers, and access to national earned income).

In this context, a crucial indicator – possibly *the* most crucial indicator – of a reduction in poverty and in gender inequality is that of gender shares of national earned income (which may reflect access to better-paid and perhaps more strategic decision-making positions without being sidetracked by tokenism in the small number of women offered access to such arenas). For the MDGs, the assumption is that gender equality in access to education is a primary means of redressing gender inequity in the economic spheres, including in employment. In fact, according to the UNDP, 'gender equality in education helps women secure employment outside the home and acquire political power, contributing to their agency in the public sphere' (2003, 86). This article challenges such a perspective on the basis of experience in Belize.

MDG gender indicators for Belize

Belize is located on the Caribbean coast of northern Central America, with Mexico to its north and Guatemala to its west and south. In ethnic terms it is a highly Diverse society. With a population approaching 300,000, it is the least populous Central American country. As a former British colony with a sizable Creole population, it is culturally and historically part of the English-speaking Caribbean, among which it is above the median in country size. Belize's HDI is 0.737, a fall on preceding years due to a long-overdue replacement in the HDR of a measure of adult literacy of 93 per cent, despite all national assessments of adult literacy placing it in the low 70s or lower. The rate included in the 2004 HDR is 77 per cent.[1]

As is well known, such national indices usually conceal intra-state disparities, not the least on the basis of gender. In fact, the UNDP (1996, 33–4) has drawn several conclusions from its production of the GDI and GEM:

- No society treats its women as well as it treats its men (no country's GDI matches its HDI).[2]

- Removing gender inequalities is not dependent upon having a high income.

- Gender inequality is not necessarily associated with high economic growth.

- Gender development occurs regardless of socio-economic characteristics.

This means that considerable progress in gender equality may be made without such 'preconditions' as high national income, high economic growth, a particular political ideology or cultural context. Countries with 'low' human development may nevertheless achieve such progress. (Of course, this also denies the 'need' for neo-liberalist prescriptions as a prerequisite for gendered human development.)

Improved gender equality is one of the principal MDGs, of which there are eight, accompanied by 18 'targets' and 48 'indicators' in order to measure progress towards the achievement of each of those Goals. Goal 3 is to 'promote gender equality and empower women' is accompanied by one target (Target 4) to 'eliminate gender disparity in primary and secondary education, preferably by 2005, and in all levels of education no later than 2015'. There are four indicators by which the achievement of Goal 3 is to be measured for each country:

- Indicator 9: the ratio of girls to boys in primary, secondary, and tertiary education;

- Indicator 10: the ratio of literate women to men, aged 15–24 years;

- Indicator 11: the share of women in wage employment in the non-agricultural sector;

- Indicator 12: the proportion of seats held by women in national parliaments.[3]

Indicator 9: education participation
Education participation rates highlight some of the hidden problems in properly understanding the MDG indicators. According to the HDR, Belize's combined primary, secondary, and tertiary gross enrolment ratios (2001/2 data) are 72 per cent for females and 71 per cent for males, and its net enrolment ratios (2000/1 data) of females to males are 1.00 (primary) and 1.07 (secondary). According to the Government of Belize's Education Statistical Digest, the net enrolment ratios of girls to boys in 2001 were 0.99 (primary) and 1.06 (secondary). However, this does not reflect gender disparities against girls (primary) or in favour of girls (secondary) as some may assume (see, for example, UNSD 2004b). The slightly lower ratio of girls in primary schooling is a reflection of the higher repetition rate for boys; the higher female ratio in secondary schooling is a reflection of that primary-school characteristic, as well as boys' higher drop-out rate at secondary level. These data produced by the Belize Government accord with UNICEF gross enrolment ratios of girls to boys in 2000: 0.97 and 1.08 respectively (2003, 118). Of course,

Indicator 9 does not reflect the actual proportions of boys and girls in the education system, just the number of girls relative to the number of boys, and the HDR combined gross enrolment ratios suggest a rate for Indicator 9 of 1.01. The withdrawal of boys from the education system, especially at secondary level, serves to elevate the apparent level of female participation suggested by this indicator. Nevertheless, the point remains that females have a higher rate of education outcome than do males in Belize.[4]

Indicator 10: literacy
For literacy, all available national indicators conclude that there is little or no gender disparity. The HDR puts the rate for those aged 15 years and above as 77.1 per cent for females and 76.7 per cent for males, suggesting that Indicator 10 for Belize is 1.01 (aged 15 years and over). The United Nations Statistics Division (UNSD) puts the rate for 15–24 year olds in Belize at a consistent 1.01 over the past decade at least. That is, available data suggest a small 'disparity' in favour of females.

Indicator 11: non-agricultural wage employment
The MDG gender measure of wage employment concerns the non-agricultural sector. The Central Statistical Office (CSO) conducts an annual Labour Force Survey (LFS). For the 2002 Survey (the latest for which data were available at the time of writing), the ratio of persons aged 14 years and over in non-agricultural occupations is 62.3 per cent (males) and 31.2 per cent (females). However, the figure for females is overstated with respect to actual wage-earning because, while only 0.3 per cent of employed women are in agricultural occupations, 4.3 per cent of employed women are described as being in 'unpaid family' employment, which suggests that around 4 per cent of women in non-agricultural 'wage' employment are unwaged. It therefore seems that, at best,

Indicator 11 is in the order of 0.44. This approximates UNSD data, which give a ratio of 0.41 for each of 2000 and 2001. The second half of this article gives closer scrutiny to the gender dimensions of the Belize labour market on the basis of trends in successive LFSs, given that this is argued as being an important aspect of gender equity.

Indicator 12: parliamentary seats

In a small country like Belize, the number of women parliamentarians fluctuates as a percentage but remains a minority. The issue of the extent to which this indicator is a more informative measure of gender power-sharing than the GEM or an important indicator in 'ridding' Belize of poverty is not debated here. However, it seems reasonable to suggest that visible achievements in the entry of women into, for example, political representation or corporate management have been more likely to mask continued resistance to gender equity than to signify real reform. Cosmetic or temporary 'advances' have often been mistaken for – or overtly promoted as – systemic progress in gender equity. They have not necessarily been accompanied by a sustained improvement in the position of women. Such illusions have been characteristic of economies, labour markets, and social institutions in both developed and developing countries, and reflect the limitations of the 'gender infrastructure' approach (Rao and Kelleher 2003). The 2004 figure for Belize for Indicator 12 is 9.3 per cent, and the UNSD rate over the period 1999–2002 is 7 per cent.

In summary, the emphasis of the single MDG concerning gender is on gender equality in education participation, and is the specific focus of the associated target. For Belize, there is a small tendency in favour of females in both education participation and literacy. However, Indicator 11 – concerning wage employment – suggests that education equality is not translating into vocational and income equity. Arguably, the achievement of this particular MDG by no means signifies the necessary advances in tackling issues of poverty and wealth distribution that are central to shifting gender relations in power-sharing and economic equity.

Belize's labour market: early gender characteristics

The 1991 national census reported an unemployment rate in Belize of 3.8 per cent: 4.2 per cent for men and 2.1 per cent for women. This may have seemed good news, but to anyone with any knowledge of Belize, it was clearly a gross understatement.

In the absence of alternative sources of data at that time, the Chief Statistician computed new estimates of unemployment, based on an assumption that Belize's labour-force participation rate equated with the average for the English-speaking Caribbean.[5] This yielded an unemployment rate of 19.6 per cent: much higher than that of the census. More importantly, it highlighted the limitations of the census in providing satisfactory measures of the labour market and strengthened the focus on the need for a more methodical collection of such data.

In 1993, the CSO conducted an LFS in each of April and October, supported by the Organization of American States and the International Labour Organization (ILO). This was the first in-depth study of the Belize labour force in ten years. The Survey followed standard international concepts and definitions set down in UN Statistical Office and ILO guidelines.

For statistical utility, it was necessary to survey 8 per cent of households country-wide, selected according to sampling by districts according to size, based on the 1991 census. This resulted in more than 3,400 households being interviewed in each of April and October. The response rate for the Survey was 86 per cent (88 per cent in April and 83 per cent in October); the 1983 rate had been 83 per cent. Subsequent surveys have been conducted on a similar basis, but confined to April only in each year, due to resource constraints. There was no survey conducted in 2000 due to the competing demands of conducting the national census. (As a consequence, all data in this article are for April in each year, with no data for 2000.)

LFS data are periodically published by the CSO, and are available for researchers and policy analysts.[6] Of course, this has been no guarantee that such data are used for such purposes, but the foundations exist for doing so. (In addition to decadal national censuses, the CSO regularly conducts and publishes a range of other surveys, more notably household surveys and 'family health' surveys – each with full attention to sex-based and gender-based dimensions – which extend the quantitative framework for planning in that country.)

It is normally the case in any country that politicians and the media give most attention to three labour-force statistics: the rise or fall in jobs, the rate of unemployment, and the rise or fall in the number of people who are unemployed. In all three cases, the 1993 Survey, on the surface, presented welcome news: between 1983 and 1993, the labour force in Belize grew by 47.6 per cent, the rate of unemployment fell by 4.2 percentage points (to 9.8 per cent), and the number of people unemployed fell by 2.8 per cent.[7]

However, in all three cases, those data concealed serious problems in terms of gender patterns. A 1994 examination of the 1983 and 1993 Surveys made a number of observations about the gendered behaviour of the Belize labour market (Johnson 1994). While the censuses had yielded female unemployment rates of a half of that for men, the 1993 LFS showed that the rate for women was at least double that for men, as well as revealing an unemployment rate treble that of the 1991 census.

In terms of sheer volume, the two largest changes between 1983 and 1993 were in the numbers of women not in the labour force and the numbers of men in employment. Despite a 40.7 per cent increase in the number of people in the Belize labour force, the female share of the labour force fell marginally to 31.8 per cent. While women's share of employment rose marginally to 30.1 per cent, women primarily responded to the behaviour of the labour market by reducing their labour-force participation rate (a fall of 5.3 percentage points to 35.0 per cent, compared with a 2.2 percentage point fall for men to 79.4 per cent) and retreated into unpaid domestic labour in even larger numbers.

On the basis of the 1983 and 1993 Surveys, the 1994 examination noted the following points:

- The female labour force was more highly educated but less well paid, less likely to be employed, and more likely to experience long-term unemployment than the male labour force.

- Men gained fully two-thirds (66.9 per cent) of the jobs added to the Belize labour market in that decade, thus exacerbating an already inequitable situation.

- Women responded to being denied equitable access to the labour market by withdrawing in large numbers: the net addition over that decade of women of working age was concentrated in the growing numbers engaged in 'home duties'.

- The fall in male unemployment was primarily a result of them benefiting most from the decade's jobs growth, while the fall in female unemployment essentially reflected them giving up on the labour market (often referred to as 'hidden unemployment').

Belize's labour market over the past decade

Between 1993 and 2002, the employed Belize labour force grew by 37.7 per cent. Over that period, there appears to have been no improved gender equity in the labour market, which suggests that the deterioration in the situation for women (especially their withdrawal from the labour force over the previous decade, particularly into home duties) has become a structural change.

Women are still unemployed at a rate that is more than double that of men (for 2002, 16.3 per cent and 7.8 per cent respectively), despite still having a labour-force participation rate less than half that of men (37.5 per cent compared with 78.8 per cent). ('Despite', because it is often normal for the labour-force participation rate to change to achieve some sort of equilibrium: a population denied job opportunities would be more inclined to withdraw from the labour market.) High unemployment and low labour-force participation indicate a greater tenacity by many women in their attempts to secure paid employment.

Women are at a multiple disadvantage here: if they don't give up and withdraw from the labour force, then they are more likely to suffer unemployment; if they find employment, it is more likely to be less well paid – especially given their higher education levels – than that for men. Men continue to hold almost 70 per cent of available jobs (women's share in 2002 was 31.0 per cent). Women also continue to bear the greater burden of long-term unemployment (at least 12 months' duration): although those rates fluctuate annually, the rate for women over the decade was a fairly constant average of at least 50 per cent higher than the male rate: another indicator of their tenacity in seeking work.

Women also continue to comprise approximately three-quarters of all persons not in the labour force (that is, persons who have left formal full-time education but do not consider themselves to be in the labour force, whether employed or unemployed). Approximately 67 per cent of such women continue to be in 'home/family duties', compared with a fairly static 3 per cent of men.

Apart from the much higher 'home duties' rate for females, other gender disparities for this group are the higher numbers of men than women who declare themselves to be in retirement (reflecting their historically higher shares of employment) and the growth over the decade in the number of women who declare that they do not 'want' to work. Over the past decade, this latter group rose from 1.2 per cent (1993) to 4.9 per cent (2002) of women not in the labour force. Given that women persist in their efforts to secure employment (as noted earlier), this trend – as with the growth over the previous decade in women withdrawing from the labour force into home duties – suggests another refuge for the 'hidden unemployed': another group of what is termed 'discouraged job seekers'.

A consideration of the data for young people (14–25 year olds) does not give much reason for optimism in the foreseeable future. Between 1993 and 2001 (2002 data for young people appear to suffer errors), the unemployment rate for young females ranged between 1.5 and 2.3 times the young male rate, standing at 32.6 per cent and 15.1 per cent respectively in 2001.[8] The labour-force participation rate seems to have risen for young females, from around 50 per cent to about 60 per cent of the male rate. As with the total adult workforce, young women continue to receive around 31 per cent of 'youth jobs', which suggests no improvement as young educated females enter the workforce.

In fact, there also appears to be a marked increase in the proportion of females in post-secondary education over the past decade. While any increase for young males is unclear from the LFS data, that for young females may indicate deferred labour-force entry due to lack of job opportunities. In 1993, 4.0 per cent of young males and 4.6 per cent of young females were in post-secondary education, and the corresponding rates in 2001 were 4.8 per cent and 8.1 per cent. If post-secondary education participation is to be encouraged, intervention is essential to ensure no labour-market resistance to young graduates.

The labour force continues to exhibit gender disparities with respect to education levels. Males in the labour force who had at least a secondary education ranged around the 19–23 per cent rate (22.6 per cent in 2001). The female equivalent was in the range of 36–43 per cent (36.4 per cent in 2001). Of the unemployed in 2001, 24.0 per cent of females had at least a secondary education, compared with 16.0 per cent of men.

If the education levels of females have evidently not assisted their achievement of equity in the labour market, they have similarly not assisted their parallel access to income equity. This is most apparent from reference to HDR GEM data, which include gender shares of earned income. The HDR presents such data for 153 countries. Belize's ratio of estimated female to male earned income is 0.24, exceeded in disparity by only two other countries— Oman (0.22) and Saudi Arabia (0.21). Of course, care needs to be taken in interstate comparisons: the estimated earned income levels of women in Oman and Saudi Arabia are 71 per cent and 61 per cent higher respectively than that of women in Belize.[9] In summary, the Belize male share of earned income is 4.1 times that for women, which is at the most inequitable end of the global spectrum: women in states with higher distributional inequality receive substantially higher incomes than their Belizean counterparts.

Concluding comments

The trickle of benefits from economic growth to those living in poverty has enabled the systemic barriers to sustainable poverty reduction to be largely left intact. For women, this is doubly disastrous, given the domestic and social spheres where power relations operate to their disadvantage: *condition* may improve, but *position* is largely left unchanged.

Like economic growth and poverty, the achievement of gender equality in education in Belize may be a necessary basis for tackling serious gender inequity in wealth distribution and economic power, but it is clearly not a sufficient basis for doing so. Education equality appears to leave the inequitable position of women unchanged in the absence of other measures that are not reflected in the MDGs.

The resistance of the Belize labour market to greater gender equality occurs despite the fact that Belizean women are, compared with Belizean men, better educated. Nevertheless, Belizean women continue to suffer twice the unemployment rate, and access fewer than one-third of the available jobs, compared with their male counterparts. And there does not appear to be a basis for optimism when considering such data for younger Belizean males and females over at least the past decade.

Successive annual labour-market data suggest that apparent gender discrimination in the Belize labour market led to a marked withdrawal of women from the labour force into unpaid domestic labour in the decade to 1993. Those data further suggest that such withdrawal has become a structural feature over the past decade, which saw no improvement in women's rate of access to paid employment, despite their higher education levels, and labour-force participation rates continuing to be a half of the male rate.

This is not to say that the government of Belize has taken no corrective measures: on the contrary. Government policy reforms in this regard in recent years have been primarily of a redistributive nature, reinforced by changes to various laws (Johnson 2002). This seems to be the very least that needs to be done (Dagdeviren *et al.* 2002), given that Belizean males receive 80 per cent of national earned income. It is, however, to challenge the adequacy – even relevance – of the single MDG concerning gender in measuring real national advances in poverty reduction and economic empowerment.[10]

In this context, the MDGs – as a framework 'adopted by a consensus of experts from the United Nations Secretariat and IMF, OECD and the World Bank' (UNSD 2004a) – avoid any systemic changes in global or national economic and political power relationships necessary to enabling real advances in gender equity. Accordingly, it is most unlikely that the achievement of the MDGs (even if that were to occur, in contrast to other global compacts) will result in any sustainable improvements in the equitable treatment of women, and therefore it can – at best – be expected to make little real impact in 'ridding' the world of poverty.

Of course, the education of girls, with particular emphasis on poor families and communities, is absolutely essential: essential in guaranteeing rights to all, essential in overcoming gender inequalities, essential in combating poverty, essential in optimising human development and well-being.[11] But it must be accompanied by deep systemic changes:

> Eliminating gender inequality in education will only work if it is part of a much broader nationwide mobilization that has ambitious goals to ensure that women fully and equally participate in all aspects of economic, social and political development.
> (Oxfam UK 2003, 29)

To return to an earlier theme: while the education of girls and women is necessary in improving the *condition* of women, it is not enough on its own to redress the inequitable *position* of women. The failure of the MDGs may not only lie in the fact that (according to early reports) donor states have failed, yet again, to meet their resource commitments to developing states (most notably, in such areas as meeting the education targets). It may also emanate from a failure, yet again, to explicitly address the systemic barriers to gender equity, even for those states that are able to meet MDG targets.

As such, the MDGs may enable many desirable goals to be attained (including necessary improvements in gender equity in schooling), but they are unlikely to be a sufficient condition to advance the position of girls and women. In this regard at least, the MDGs appear to be in danger of becoming yet another lost opportunity in global development effort.

Robert Johnson is a development consultant currently engaged as a UN adviser on human-rights treaty reporting to the Government of Timor-Leste. He was social policy adviser to the Government of Belize 1993–5, and a human-development consultant in Belize 2001–3. Contact: rj_bz@yahoo.com.

Notes

1 Unless otherwise apparent, all references in this article to HDR data are to UNDP (2004).

2 According to UNDP (2003), Germany was a single exception, with GDI>HDI; for the 2004 HDR, two countries (Sweden and Latvia) achieved GDI=HDI.

3 The primary reference for MDG information, and especially for technical data on indicators and available country-based data, is UNSD (2004a): for country data, follow the link for the relevant indicator. For Goal 3, reference should also be made to UNSD (2004b). References in this section to UNSD data for MSG Indicators for Belize are to UNSD (2004a).

4 Watkins produces an Education Performance Index for 104 developing countries: a composite of net enrolment rate, completion rate, and female:male enrolment ratio. Belize is ranked 49th (in descending order of performance), due to a poor completion rate (=74th) and despite a high net enrolment rate (=15th). Only 11 countries out-perform its female:male ratio (viz. for those countries with at least 96 per cent female enrolment and a male–female ratio no greater than 1 per cent) (Watkins 2000, 348–50).

5 While Belize is geographically located within Central America, its British colonial heritage and ethnic composition have more closely tied it to English-speaking Caribbean states. This statistical assumption was made on that basis, although the entry of many Central Americans into Belize in the late 1980s and early 1990s due to civil conflicts in the region rapidly changed Belize's ethnic and cultural profile. Even so, the subsequent LFS series supports the Chief Statistician's initial assumption.

6 The co-operation of the CSO and, in particular, its Deputy Chief Statistician, Elizabeth Arnold, in providing annual LFS data to the author is gratefully acknowledged. Any errors in interpretation of those data are entirely the responsibility of the author.

7 References are to the average of the data for each of the April and October Surveys in 1993, as a better point of comparison with the 1983 data.

8 Indicator 45 of the MDGs is the only other indicator to provide for sex-disaggregated data: for the unemployment rate of 15–24 year olds. For some reason, this concerns Goal 8: 'develop a global partnership for development'.

9 Refer to UNDP (2004), GEM Table 25, pages 221–4. Data need to be treated with caution on account of their rather vague derivation. The ratio of estimated female to male earned income is derived from the data for estimated earned income in Table 24 (GDI) which 'are crudely estimated on the basis of [various data] for the most recent year available during 1991–2000' (Note c to Table 24; Note c to Table 25 says '1991–2001').

10 The need for the MDGs to take due account of gender dimensions of economic equity and poverty appears to be acknowledged by the UN, with some apparent belated realisation of the effort required. In a section dealing with improving the quality of MDG data concerning 'poverty and income distribution', an Economic and Social Council paper notes that '[t]he need for gender analysis of income and consumption and of intra-household distribution is also well established but evidently requires a major long-term effort' (UN Statistical Commission 2004, 17).

11 It is also essential in preventing the deaths of children. Watkins argues the presence of 'gender apartheid' in education, with young girls bearing the brunt of the widespread denial of access to schooling and of high child mortality rates; he identifies overcoming the former as one prerequisite for tackling the latter (Watkins 2000, 2–3).

References

Dagdeviren, H., R. van der Hoeven, and J. Weeks (2002) 'Poverty reduction with growth and redistribution', *Development and Change* 33(3): 383–413

Economic Commission for Latin America and the Caribbean (1997) *Caribbean Social Structures and the Changing World of Men*, with the Caribbean Development and Cooperation Committee

Gaiha, R. (2003) 'Are Millennium goals of poverty reduction useful?', *Oxford Development Studies* 31(1): 59–84

Johnson, R. (1994) 'Is there Resistance to Gender Equity in the Labour Market? Indicators from the National Labour Force Survey', paper presented to the Annual Conference on Belizean Studies, Society for the Promotion of Education and Research, Belize City, Belize, 1994

Johnson, R. (2002) 'Women's economic development: Belize's progress towards an elusive goal', *IDEAS* 7(3): 6–8, Society for the Promotion of Education and Research, Belize City, Belize

Monbiot, G. (2003) *The Age of Consent: A Manifesto for a New World Order*, London: Flamingo

Nederveen Pieterse, J. (2002) 'Global inequality: bringing politics back in', *Third World Quarterly* 23(6): 1023–46

Oxfam UK (2003) 'A Fair Chance: Attaining Gender Equality in Basic Education by 2005',http://oxfam.org.uk/ what_we_do/issues/education/ downloads/gce_afairchance.pdf (last checked by the author November 2004)

Rao, A. and D. Kelleher (2003) 'Institutions, organisations and gender equality in an era of globalisation', *Gender and Development* 11(1): 142–8

UNDP (1996) *Human Development Report*, New York: Oxford University Press

UNDP (2003) *Human Development Report*, New York: Oxford University Press

UNDP (2004) *Human Development Report*, New York: Oxford University Press

UNICEF (2003) *The State of the World's Children 2004*, New York: UNICEF

UNSD (2004a) 'Millennium Indicators Database', http://millenniumindicators.un.org/ unsd/mi/mi_goals.asp (last checked by the author November 2004)

UNSD (2004b) 'Progress towards the MDGs, 1990–2003: Summary', http://millenniumindicators.un.org/unsd/mi/ mi_coverfinal.htm (last checked by the author November 2004)

UN Statistical Commission (2004) 'Indicators for Monitoring the Implementation of the Millennium Development Goals', UN Economic and Social Council E/CN.3/2004/23, http://unstats.un.org/unsd/statcom/doc04/20 04-23e.pdf (last checked by the author March 2005)

Watkins, K. (2000) 'The Oxfam Education Report', www.oxfam.org.uk/ what_you_can_do/campaign/mdg/ downloads/edreport/edreport.htm (last checked by the author November 2004)

Out of the margins: the MDGs through a CEDAW lens

Ceri Hayes

This article examines the Millennium Development Goals (MDGs) from a women's human rights perspective. It outlines some of the practical ways in which human rights principles, and the provisions set out in the Convention on the Elimination of All Forms of Discrimination Against Women (CEDAW) in particular, can be used to ensure that the MDGs are met in a way that respects and promotes gender equality and women's human rights.[1]

The inclusion of the goal to 'promote gender equality and empower women' (Goal 3) in the MDGs demonstrates the impact of many years of lobbying by the women's movement to promote gender equality and women's human rights in development. Nevertheless, many gender activists have expressed concern that the MDGs fail to represent the vision and commitment to gender equality and women's empowerment that are set out in key human rights instruments, such as CEDAW, and outcome documents of intergovernment conferences of the 1990s. The most notable of these outcome documents is the Beijing Declaration and Platform for Action (1995).

Given that the MDGs now play a central role in shaping development policy and practice nationally and internationally, women's human rights organisations, such as WOMANKIND Worldwide, have had to ask themselves how they might use the Goals to further the agenda of the international women's movement.

This article examines how CEDAW, and some of the other tools available to the CEDAW Committee, such as the CEDAW reporting mechanism and the Committee's General Recommendations, which elaborate the Committee's view of the obligations assumed under the Convention, can be used to enhance and strengthen efforts to meet the MDGs by addressing gender inequality as one of the underlying causes of poverty. CEDAW is one of a number of legal instruments that have, over the years, elaborated upon the nature and scope of women's human rights. It is the only international human rights treaty to comprehensively address the issue of women's human rights. CEDAW needs to be considered in the context of other global human rights instruments, including the Beijing Platform for Action and the International Covenant on Economic, Social and Cultural Rights (1966). In this context, the provisions of CEDAW on women's human rights look considerably stronger than they do alone.

The article begins with a brief consideration of the challenges, opportunities, and paradoxes presented by the MDGs, from a women's human rights perspective. It then examines how the MDGs sit within the broader human rights agenda.

The final section focuses on CEDAW and the practical ways in which the Convention can inform and guide strategies for the implementation of the Goals to ensure that women and men benefit equally from development gains.

The MDGs: challenges, opportunities, and paradoxes

Adopted by the Heads of State and Government in September 2000, the Millennium Declaration (UN 2000) shares CEDAW's vision of a world where women and men are equal. It identifies gender equality as an essential ingredient for achieving all the MDGs and affirms the need to combat violence against women and to implement CEDAW.

Yet, this vision is not embraced by the MDGs themselves, or by the limited and (for the most part) gender-blind selection of targets and indicators chosen to monitor progress towards their fulfilment. Even Goal 3 has been interpreted in the narrowest sense, with a focus on the target of educational access to the exclusion of other barriers to gender equality, such as the devastating impact that gender-based violence has on women's lives. It also fails to take into account the fact that in some countries, particularly in Latin America, gender parity in education has already been attained and yet gender inequality is still a feature of these societies.

It is, of course, impossible to expect a set of universal goals to take account of the many differences between countries. In practice, efforts have been made to establish complementary goals and targets and to 'localise' the MDGs (that is, to interpret them in a way that reflects national and local development priorities and agendas). There is still a long way to go until the attainment of gender inequality and (in particular) the realisation of women's human rights are seen as cross-cutting issues in the implementation of the Goals, but there are some examples of good practice.

One example is that the UNDP has been at the forefront of MDG 'scorekeeping' at the country level and has worked with governments and civil society to ensure that gender issues are built into the national Millennium Development Goal Reports (MDGRs). For instance, in Albania, a thematic Working Group on Gender was formed to establish a baseline against which to measure progress towards meeting the Goals. The process involved consultation with more than 650 stakeholders from all over Albania and has greatly enhanced national ownership of the process. It has also allowed the Goals to be translated into targets and indicators that are most appropriate for women at the sub-national level (UNDP Albania 2004) .

Also at the national level, some countries, such as Viet Nam, have used their National Plan of Action for the Advancement of Women as the basis for identifying targets and indicators towards meeting Goal 3 (UN in Viet Nam 2002), but this seems to be the exception rather than the norm. Given how far the MDGR process has advanced, national-level reporting does represent the best opportunity to build national commitment to women's rights and gender equality; but these processes must, of course, be accompanied by sufficient political will and resources. The MDGs do have broad support among governments and can offer gender activists the potential of a new impetus for old agendas, but existing approaches to implementation must be revised if the MDGs are not to reinforce traditional top–down approaches to development and add another layer of 'invisibilisation' for women.

Another example is at the international level. The UN Millennium Project's Task Force on Education and Gender Equality has produced a series of recommendations to strengthen the implementation of Goal 3, including a set of six strategic priorities, such as the guarantee of sexual and reproductive health rights for girls and women, and an end to violence against women (Birdsall *et al.* 2004).

The MDGs and human rights

While the Millennium Declaration reaffirms states' commitment to promote human rights, the MDGs make no specific reference to human rights. Nevertheless, they do reflect a human rights agenda. Goal 1, for example, sets out time-bound targets for reducing poverty, one of the greatest denials of human rights. Also, Goals 4 (to reduce child mortality), 5 (to improve maternal health), and 6 (to combat HIV/AIDS, malaria, and other diseases) can be compared to the human right to health, set out in the core human rights treaties.

However, it is dangerous to assume that the MDGs will automatically contribute to the promotion of respect for human rights simply by addressing thematic human rights concerns (Committee on Economic, Social and Cultural Rights 1990). The case of China, which has seen impressive economic growth in recent years yet has an estimated 30m women 'missing' as a result of sex-selective abortions and infanticide (Seager 2003), highlights how a country can make progress towards the poverty-reduction goal while violations of women's human rights continue.

International human rights rest on a series of core principles, including equality, non-discrimination, and the fact that human rights are interdependent, i.e. equal attention must be given to the realisation of all rights. Thus, a human rights approach would forbid trade-offs being made by decision makers between economic growth and gender equality. It reminds us that progress in development can be measured only by improvements in the lives of *all* individuals.

A human rights approach would place as much emphasis on the importance of *process* as it does on outcome. For instance, the human rights principles of participation and empowerment demand the meaningful involvement of poor people in all stages of the MDG process, while the principle of accountability underlines the rights of populations to monitor the progress of governments towards meeting the Goals, and to hold them to account where they fail. Given that poor women tend to be excluded twice over – on the grounds of poverty and gender – their involvement in these processes is crucial if all the Goals are to be achieved. Thus, a human rights approach positions poor women as key actors in the development process, rather than as passive recipients of aid. Yet the involvement of poor women – and the involvement of civil society more generally – in the MDG process has been largely peripheral to date. At the national level, the MDGs remain the principal tool for participating in the MDG process and for holding governments to account. It is therefore essential that they are made accessible to everyone, including the poorest and most marginalised people, and that these people are empowered to participate meaningfully in the reporting and monitoring process.

More and better access to information and data concerning the Goals would, of course, not, by itself, achieve women's empowerment. The Goals must also seek to address the nature of gender relations and the environment in which women exercise their agency. This means tackling the inequality and the denial of rights at all levels, including the macro-economic structures, the political institutions, and the cultural practices and attitudes that sustain forms of discrimination.

Of course, just as we cannot assume that the attainment of the MDGs would inevitably contribute to the promotion of human rights, neither can we suppose that a commitment by governments to apply human rights principles to policy making would necessarily contribute to the realisation of the MDGs. The ratification of international human rights treaties has not generally resulted in dramatic improvements in the quality of the lives of citizens. The gap between the rhetoric of human rights and the reality of failure to uphold them is particularly marked in the case of women's rights. For human rights principles to be truly effective, action is required on a number of different levels. In the context of the struggle for gender equality, it means incorporating international human rights norms, set out in instruments such as CEDAW, into national constitutions and laws. It also means investing in national equality commissions and human rights bodies, education and outreach programmes for both women and men, and developing and providing access to fair arbitration systems at the local level. This costs money, and, in the context of the MDGs, there needs to be far greater emphasis on financing these systems of implementation, to render the Goals effective. There also needs to be a broader discussion about the meaning and practical implications of a rights-based approach to the MDG process among governments, civil society, the private sector, and international financial institutions.

The MDGs through a CEDAW lens

This section focuses on how the standards and principles set out in CEDAW can be used to strengthen existing approaches to the MDGs and reinforce the processes for achieving the Goals.

A number of arguments have already been made which support the rationale for adopting a more gender-sensitive approach to the MDGs, but these primarily advance an 'instrumentalist' logic that seeks to convince the economists of the *effectiveness* of mainstreaming gender. That is, they are based on the rationale that attempting to achieve the MDGs without promoting gender equality and women's rights will both raise the costs and decrease the likelihood of achieving the Goals (Carlsson and Valdivieso 2003).

Looking at the MDGs through a CEDAW lens adds another dimension to these arguments. The Convention rests on the conviction that all women have human *rights*, not just *needs*. Seen in this light, the ideals of equality and non-discrimination are, in fact, important ends in themselves, not simply means of delivering the MDGs in a cost-effective way. CEDAW also identifies the factors that give rise to inequality, thus preventing the realisation of the MDGs, and highlights some of the solutions required to address them.

The Convention covers a range of areas relevant to the MDGs, such as education, employment, and maternal mortality, but there are also gaps. The General Recommendations and Concluding Comments of the CEDAW Committee help to close some of these gaps, providing as they do more detailed guidance for tackling barriers to gender equality and women's empowerment. In addition, both the official reporting process and the shadow reporting process that monitor states' compliance with the Convention offer opportunities for dialogue between states, the CEDAW Committee, and NGOs, which can be used to explore and strengthen the links between women's human rights and specific Goals.

Since the scope of this article precludes an analysis of all of the MDGs through a CEDAW lens, the next section examines just two of the MDGs: Goal 1 and Goal 3. They are closely interrelated, and the pathways for achieving them intersect and complement each other. The analysis aims to highlight some of the specific interventions and policy choices that would be required for a CEDAW-compliant approach to these particular Goals.

Meeting Goal 1

The targets for Goal 1 include halving the proportion of people whose income is less than US$1 a day, and halving the proportion of people who suffer from hunger by 2015. Yet low income and hunger are just two manifestations of this complex phenomenon, which includes lack of clothing and lack of access to education, health care, and social services. Goal 1 also fails to take into account the gender dimensions of poverty and the different ways in which economic poverty affects women's and men's lives.

The consequences of this approach can be seen in a sample of MDG Reports that were analysed for the UNDP. Just two out of 13 national reports (those of Mozambique and Viet Nam) include gender analyses of the causes and impact of women's poverty, and only one report (Bolivia) makes a connection between the concerns of reducing poverty, increasing opportunities for women, and ensuring their human rights (Menon-Sen 2003, 8).

What CEDAW says

While there is no provision in the Convention that addresses poverty specifically, CEDAW identifies gender-specific obstacles to the equal enjoyment of rights and freedoms, all of which are relevant, in one way or another, to eliminating women's poverty; for example, discriminatory cultural patterns and customary practices (Article 5), women's exclusion from political decision-making (Articles 7 and 8), and discrimination in the fields of education (Article 10), health (Article 12), property ownership (Article 15), and in marriage and family matters (Article 16). The language of Article 14, which addresses the problems faced by rural women, is particularly sensitive to women's vulnerability to poverty.

The CEDAW preamble highlights women's particular vulnerability to violations of their human rights in situations of poverty. Its reaffirmation of the indivisibility of rights underlines the importance of holistic, multi-dimensional approaches to tackling the goal of poverty reduction, since women without adequate economic resources are unlikely to be able to enjoy their other rights, such as control over resources such as housing and food.

Equally, women without freedom of expression are unlikely to be able to fight for their most basic needs. By positioning women as people with their own rights, rather than as dependants of male relatives, CEDAW demands that attention should be paid to the processes that allow women to claim their rights. Thus, women should have the right to participate in the design of strategies to eradicate poverty on equal terms with men.

The two layers of discrimination against women – discrimination contained in laws and discrimination stemming from procedures, policies, or practice – that the Convention identifies are also helpful, in that they illustrate the different types of strategy required to reach Goal 1. For instance, inheritance rights that provide only for sons are an example of *de jure* discrimination that can plunge women even further into poverty, unless suitable legal reforms are carried out. The unequal workload and responsibilities of many rural women are examples of *de facto* discrimination, which need to be addressed by awareness-raising and a change of attitudes.

A more detailed analysis of the provisions set out in CEDAW and the CEDAW Committee's various instruments highlights a number of ways in which the implementation of the MDGs can be strengthened. These translate into three strategic action points, and a series of practical steps. The latter can act as a checklist for national-level activities to ensure that measures undertaken to meet Goal 1 of the MDGs advance gender equality and women's human rights. The strategic action points are addressed in the three sections that follow.

Table 1: Relevant CEDAW provisions

Article 5	Modification of social and cultural patterns that promote stereotypes
Article 10c	Elimination of stereotyped concepts at all levels of education, including textbooks, teaching methods
Article 11:1e	Right to social security
Article 11:2c	Provision of social services
Article 13a	Right to family benefits
Article 14:2c	Right of rural women to benefit from social security programmes
Article 14:2h	Right to enjoy adequate living conditions
General Recommendation 16	Unpaid women workers in rural and urban family enterprises
General Recommendation 23, paragraphs 12 and 17	Discriminatory laws and customs that prevent women from having equal access to resources; that accord husband the status of head of household and primary decision maker

1 To ensure that national development strategies strengthen the substantive rights of poor women and do not discriminate against them

CEDAW cautions against the kind of stereotyping that depicts women as mothers and wives only, and results in analysis in which they appear only in relation to issues such as children and health. It calls for their full and equal participation in public life. Therefore, any strategy to achieve Goal 1 must take into consideration the views and priorities of women and should militate against restricting interventions to the areas of education and health, to the exclusion of other areas such as employment, social positioning, and violence against women. Moreover, it is no defence to say that the prevailing culture of a country portrays women as the dependants of men, since CEDAW calls on all states to modify social and cultural patterns that promote stereotypes.

The CEDAW approach also rules out pursuing strategies for reducing income-poverty if these violate women's human rights. For instance, while the growth of textile and garment factories in countries such as Indonesia has allowed some women to gain an advantage in terms of income, this expansion of so-called 'women's jobs' has disproportionately sidelined women in temporary work with few workers' rights. In some situations, women are reported to have been subjected to sexual harassment, coerced into working overtime, and punished when they work slowly (Global Alliance for Workers and Communities 2001)

Projects such as UNIFEM's DESafios in Latin America, which takes a rights-based approach to women's economic and social rights, offer a practical illustration of how women's role in development can be strengthened by building their capacity to monitor the allocation of resources for the fulfilment of government commitments, promoting their political participation in economic decisions and supporting women's organisations and trade unions (UNIFEM 2003, 28).

MDG strategies should therefore:

- ensure that national-level targets and strategies are set/revised in consultation with women living in poverty and/or with the NGOs that represent them;

- ensure that strategies to meet all the MDGs measure the impact and improvements for poor women and devise sub-targets that take into consideration the most marginalised groups of poor women, such as widows, and rural and disabled women;

• describe the types of policy formulation in which women have participated and the level and extent of their participation;

• provide for education and training to ensure that women are fully informed of the MDG process.

2 To reform laws and policies to secure women's equal access to economic resources
One of the biggest constraints preventing women from accessing employment and income is their unequal access to capital, resources – particularly land and credit – and labour markets. This has a direct impact on their ability to provide security against hunger and poverty. Women's equality in accessing employment and income is directly linked to their empowerment and their ability to participate fully in the economic and social lives of their country. This illustrates clearly how progress towards Goal 1 is dependent on progress towards Goal 3, and vice versa.

CEDAW emphasises the legal steps required to secure women's equal access to economic resources. For instance, on the question of women's land rights, CEDAW draws attention to the legal *process* through which land reform is secured and the need to remove barriers that restrict women's legal capacity in any way (CEDAW 1979, Article 15). Strategies to meet Goal 1 must therefore incorporate measures to strengthen women's legal aid and to reform the justice system, if women are to claim their equal property rights.

An initiative between civil society organisations and regional government officials in the Western Cape region of South Africa used CEDAW as a baseline for measuring the extent of the exclusion of rural women farm workers from economic opportunities. This enabled participants to identify the gender issues that compounded women's experience of poverty. This work contributed to the development of gender-sensitive indicators for monitoring the progress of rural women in other regions (International Center for Research on Women 2002).

MDG strategies should:

• improve legal aid and education for women seeking redress on poverty issues;

Table 2: Relevant CEDAW provisions

Article 2c	Establish legal protection of rights of women on equal basis with men
Article 11:1b	Same employment opportunities as men
Article 11:1d	Equal pay for equal work
Article 13b	Right to bank loans, mortgages, and other forms of financial credit
Article 14:2g	Access to agricultural credit and loans
Article 15:2	Equal rights to conclude contracts and administer property
Article 16:1h	Equal rights to ownership of property
General Recommendation 13	Equal remuneration for work of equal value
General Recommendation 17	Measurement and quantification of unremunerated domestic activities of women and their recognition in the GNP
General Recommendation 21	Equality in marriage and family relations

- include steps to reform the justice system and make it more accessible to women;

- measure compliance with CEDAW on women's access to economic assets;

- measure reductions in gender disparities in access to, and control over, economic resources, including the right to inheritance and land ownership;

- ensure that women have access to financial services, improve availability of credit, and support innovative lending practices;

- support self-help initiatives of poor women, such as co-operatives, that seek to develop work opportunities in their communities.

3 To improve measurement and monitoring of women's poverty and their access to information

General Recommendation 9 of the CEDAW Committee points to the need for reliable data disaggregated by sex in order to understand 'the real situation for women' (Committee on the Elimination of Discrimination Against Women 1990). In a number of its Concluding Comments (the remarks and recommendations made by the Committee at the end of the reporting process), it has also urged states to assess the gender impact of anti-poverty measures (Committee on the Elimination of Discrimination Against Women 2003, paragraph 34).

Access to data and other information is critical if women are to be given the opportunity to make informed choices about their lives, to challenge the status quo, and to hold governments and individuals accountable. However, apart from some notable exceptions,[2] there is currently a huge gap in the quality and quantity of data available for monitoring the extent of women's poverty. The lack of information available to poor women about poverty-reduction strategies, and their rights more generally, also constitutes a form of discrimination. This must be addressed urgently if Goal 1 is to be met.

MDG strategies should:

- conduct assessments of their impact, disaggregated by sex, with a view to eliminating discriminatory practices that affect women's economic and other interests;

- improve the availability and quality of sex-disaggregated poverty data on, for instance, minimum wage levels and equal pay for equal work requirements, in order to stabilise women's income levels above the poverty line;

- ensure that strategies to achieve Goal 1 include various awareness-raising initiatives, such as skills-training workshops and media information campaigns.

Table 3: Relevant CEDAW provisions

Article 10h	Access to educational information to ensure health and well-being of families
Article 14:2b	Access to adequate health-care facilities, including information
General Recommendation 9	Statistical data concerning the situation of women
General Recommendation 17	Measurement and quantification of the unremunerated domestic activities of women and their recognition in the GNP
General Recommendation 24, paragraph 9	States must report on their legislation, plans, and policies for women with reliable data disaggregated by sex

Meeting Goal 3

If Goal 3 is examined from the point of view of women's human rights as enshrined in CEDAW, it is clear (as pointed out in detail in other articles in this collection) that the target of eliminating gender disparity in access to education is far from adequate to address the scope of inequality women face. The Convention recommends a holistic approach to tackling discrimination, including the need to ensure equal opportunities for women and men. It places equal emphasis on the importance of targeting culture and tradition and sexual harassment and stereotyping, underlining the fact that women's empowerment and the achievement of gender equality are not just goals but *processes*.

The next section examines and provides recommendations for two areas that have received little attention to date in the MDGRs – gender equality in the labour market and violence against women – but which are, according to CEDAW, equally critical to the achievement of gender equality and women's empowerment.

Gender equality in the labour market: what CEDAW says

One of the indicators for achieving Goal 3 is women's share of wage employment in the non-agricultural sector. This can be used to measure progress in women's economic opportunity, but it has its drawbacks. For instance, it may fail to distinguish between different types of work or to indicate how women's increased share of wage employment adds to their total workload (Grown *et al.* 2003).

CEDAW encourages an emphasis not only on women's right to work, but on the *quality* of their working conditions. Examples are their right to maternity leave, to the protection of their health and safety at work, and to the same pay and benefits of work as men. National indicators for Goal 3 could therefore be strengthened by including qualitative measures that are linked to concrete steps to improve the quality of women's working conditions. This might require putting temporary special measures in place, until more long-term measures can be taken.

Table 4: Relevant CEDAW provisions

Article 11	Take measures to eliminate discrimination in employment, including equal pay for work of equal value, right to social security, maternity leave
Article 13	Eliminate discrimination in areas of economic and social life
Article 14:2e	Right of rural women to organise to obtain equal access to economic opportunities through employment or self-employment
Article 16:1g	Same rights as husband to choose a profession and occupation
General Recommendation 5	Temporary special measures to advance women's integration into education, the economy, politics, and employment
General Recommendation 13	Equal remuneration for work of equal value
General Recommendation 16	Unpaid women workers in rural and urban family enterprises
General Recommendation 17	Measurement and quantification of unremunerated domestic activities of women and their recognition in the GNP
General Recommendation 19, paragraphs 18 and 24j	Sexual harassment in the workplace constitutes a health and safety issue
General Recommendation 21, paragraphs 24, 41, and 42	Equal rights of husband and wife to choose employment and need to modify stereotypes that prevent women from choosing their profession

The CEDAW Committee has drawn particular attention to the situation of particular groups of women, such as migrant workers, who are often forced into unsafe working environments if they lack proper legal status. A UNIFEM project that teaches migrant workers about their rights and advises government agencies on how to handle migrant labour demonstrates how a rights-based approach can empower women to improve their legal, social, and economic situation and can strengthen the accountability mechanisms that support them (UNIFEM 2003).

Since CEDAW prohibits stereotyping, any strategy to tackle the MDGs ought to include steps to sensitise and educate women and men and counter stereotypes that prevent women from choosing their profession, thus promoting the presence of women in many different types of careers and providing for equal labour division in the household.

MDG strategies should:

- ensure that strategies to implement Goal 3 include measures of gender equality in the labour market that reflect women's economic realities, both in the public and private sectors;

- develop sensitisation programmes for women and men to counter negative stereotypes and ensure equal opportunities in the labour market and equal division of labour in the household;

- devise sub-targets that take into consideration marginalised groups of women;

- consider temporary special measures, such as positive action, to address women's under-representation in certain areas of work and to safeguard their health and safety.

Violence against women: what CEDAW says

Although CEDAW does not make specific reference to violence against women, General Recommendation 19 of the CEDAW Committee states that the definition of discrimination includes violence against women. Violence acts as a barrier to women's empowerment and negatively affects their health, education, and employment. This has obvious implications for the MDGs. Violence against women threatens to undermine fulfilment of all the Goals. For example, women's lack of ability to negotiate the conditions in which sex takes place, free from the fear of violence, increases their vulnerability to HIV infection (relevant to Goals 3, 5, and 6). HIV infection, in turn, can compound women's poverty, as they may lose their jobs through illness or have to pay medical expenses (relevant to Goal 1).

The CEDAW Committee has underlined, in its Concluding Comments to various countries, the importance of assessing the extent and prevalence of all forms of violence against women and of introducing measures to combat the problem. Specifically, it has recommended legislation, plus comprehensive gender awareness-raising and education. It recommends the latter not only for the public in general, but

Table 5: Relevant CEDAW provisions

Article 6	Suppress all forms of trafficking and exploitation of prostitution of women
Article 11	Eliminate discrimination in employment: General Recommendation 19 recognises sexual harassment as a threat to health and safety in the workplace
Declaration on the Elimination of All Forms of Violence Against Women	Violence against women
General Recommendation 19	Violence against women

for law-enforcement agencies (such as judges, lawyers, and police officers) in particular. It also recommends the provision of shelters for women who are fleeing violence. WOMANKIND Worldwide's Nkyinkyim programme in Ghana has adopted this kind of holistic approach to tackling the problem of domestic violence, and this has proved very effective.[3]

The CEDAW Committee also holds states liable for the rights violations committed by private individuals. However, since CEDAW does not always have the same binding force as domestic law, it is important that national accountability mechanisms and community interventions are reinforced. For example, in India, the National Commission on Women has used CEDAW to draw up guidelines and norms regarding sexual harassment that have been widely circulated to government departments and is undertaking an ongoing assessment of their implementation (International Center for Research on Women 2002).

Strategies to meet Goal 3 can be strengthened at the national level by the inclusion of an indicator to monitor the prevalence of violence against women – Viet Nam has already done this – but they could also include targets for improving national and/or local mechanisms to tackle the problem.

MDG strategies should:

- adopt specific indicators to measure the quantity and quality of programmes aimed at addressing violence against women and changing social norms that tolerate violence against women;

- support the reform and full implementation of laws against family violence and abuse, rape, and sexual assault;

- harmonise strategies to eradicate poverty with strategies to tackle violence;

- promote national-level media campaigns to promote respect for women.

Conclusion: action to pursue in 2005

The MDGs are here to stay. It is crucial for women's rights activists to use all the available tools and opportunities. Hence, we need to promote better integration of a gender equality and women's human rights perspective in the MDG processes.

An important step in this process is to articulate, build, and strengthen both the conceptual and practical linkages between the implementation of the Beijing Platform for Action and the Millennium Declaration and MDGs, and to ensure that this knowledge is used to inform the 2005 review processes. In practical terms, this involves articulating and measuring the gender dimensions of each of the Goals, and ensuring, as a minimum requirement, that targets and indicators are compliant with CEDAW and other instruments, such as the Beijing Platform for Action, both at the international level and, more importantly, at the national level, using national MDGRs. It also involves integrating CEDAW reports, National Plans of Action for women, MDG country reports, and other existing development plans, as well as raising awareness and supporting the efforts of activists seeking to build bridges between these different areas.

This article has highlighted just a few of the practical ways in which human rights principles, and CEDAW in particular, can guide national-level monitoring and the processes required to meet the MDGs in a way that tackles the root causes of inequality and discrimination against women. This is something that existing approaches are failing to do. CEDAW does not have all the answers, but implementing these basic provisions would go a long way towards ensuring that the MDGs are also met.

Ceri Hayes is Policy Manager at WOMANKIND Worldwide. WOMANKIND Worldwide is a UK-based international women's human rights and development organisation, established in 1989, which works with partner organisations around the world to achieve lasting improvement in women's economic, social, and political position. Contact: ceri@womankind.org.uk; WOMANKIND Worldwide, Development House, 56–64 Leonard Street, London, EC2A 4JX, UK.

Notes

1 This article is a synthesis of a longer paper originally written in September 2003. It has subsequently been printed by WOMANKIND Worldwide and is available from ceri@womankind.org.uk. With thanks to Professor Diane Elson for the helpful discussions and guidance in researching the original paper.

2 For example, the UN Economic Commission for Latin America and the Caribbean has developed a set of gender-sensitive indicators that have been used to measure the extent of women's poverty for the whole region.

3 See www.womankind.org.uk/ four%20literacies/bodylit/wafrica.html for further information about WOMANKIND Worldwide's Nkyinkyim programme.

References

Beijing Declaration and Platform for Action, Fourth World Conference on Women, Beijing, China, UN Department of Publication Information, 1995

Birdsall, N., A. Ibrahim, and G. Rao Gupta (2004) *From Promises to Action: Recommendations for Gender Equality and the Empowerment of Women*, Millennium Project Task Force 3 Interim Report on Gender Equality, UNDP

Carlsson, H. and C. Valdivieso (2003) 'Gender Equality and the Millennium Development Goals', Gender and Development Group, World Bank

CEDAW (1979) *UN Convention on the Elimination of All Forms of Discrimination Against Women*, UN Doc. A/34/36

Committee on Economic, Social and Cultural Rights (1990) *General Comment 2, International Technical Assistance Measures*, UN Doc. HRI/GEN1/REV 1 at 45 (Fourth Session)

Committee on the Elimination of Discrimination Against Women (1990) *General Recommendation 9, Statistical Data Concerning the Situation of Women*, UN Doc. A/44/38

Committee on the Elimination of Discrimination Against Women (2003) *Concluding Comments on Canada's 5th Periodic Report*, UN Doc. CEDAW/C/2003/1/CRP.3/Add.5/Rev.1 (31 January 2003)

Global Alliance for Workers and Communities (2001) 'Workers Survey, Indonesia, Nike', www.theglobalalliance.org/workerssurveys.ht m (last checked by the author January 2005)

Grown, C., G. Rao Gupta, and Z. Khan (2003) *Promises to Keep: Achieving Gender Equality and the Empowerment of Women*, Background Paper of the Task Force on Education and Gender Equality, UNDP

International Center for Research on Women (2002) 'CEDAW: An Essential Tool for Overcoming Poverty and Ensuring the Dignity and Rights of Women', statement to the Committee on Foreign Relations of the US Senate, www.womenstreaty.org/ICRWstatement.pdf (last checked by the author January 2005)

International Covenant on Economic, Social and Cultural Rights (1966) www.unhchr.ch/html/menu3/b/a_cescr.htm (last checked by the author January 2005)

Menon-Sen, K. (2003) 'Millennium Development Goal. National Reports: A Quick Look Through A Gender Lens', UNDP, 1 United Nations Plaza, New York, NY 10017, USA www.undp.org/ gender/docs/mdgs-genderlens.pdf

Seager, J. (2003) *The Atlas of Women: An Economic, Social and Political Survey*, The Women's Press

UN (2000) 'United Nations Millennium Declaration', Ref: A/55/L.2, www.un.org/millennium/declaration/ares552e. htm (last checked by the author January 2005)

UNDP Albania (2004) *Albania National Report on Progress Toward Achieving the Millennium Development Goals*

UNIFEM (2003) 'Annual Report 2002/2003', www.unifem.org/index.php?f_page_pid+180 (last checked by the author January 2005)

UN in Viet Nam, (2002) '*Millennium Development Goals: Bringing the MDGs Closer to the People*', www.undp.org/ mdg/country_regionalreports.html#Viet%20Na m (last checked by the author January 2005)

Linking women's human rights and the MDGs:

an agenda for 2005 from the UK Gender and Development Network[1]

Genevieve Renard Painter

The Millennium Development Goals (MDGs) are a potentially powerful tool for progress on development and human rights. Women's human rights activists should recognise and build on the political will mobilised around the MDGs. However, the MDGs reflect problems in the dominant development approach. They seek to use women in their existing social roles to 'deliver' other aims, and do not address the need to eradicate gender inequality, resulting in lack of commitment to address key issues for women, including gender-based violence. There are further problems with the MDGs' indicators, analytical approach, and accountability mechanisms. The MDGs should be reframed as human rights obligations. To this end, links should be fostered between the 2005 reviews of implementation of the Beijing Platform for Action and progress on the Millennium Declaration and the MDGs.

The year 2005 is a key moment for women's human rights advocacy, because the Beijing Platform for Action (BPFA), the Millennium Declaration, and the MDGs will be reviewed.

To prepare for the 2005 reviews, the UK's Gender and Development Network (GADN) commissioned research on the conceptual and practical links between the review processes.[2] The GADN believes that the 2005 reviews are an arena for emphasising the centrality of a women's human rights approach to development. They are an opportunity to reclaim gender mainstreaming as a strategy to achieving women's human rights, grounded in treaty obligations, not a technical process for efficient progress towards development goals. Linking the Millennium Review and the Beijing+10 Review processes presents an opportunity to reframe the MDGs as international human rights obligations.

The MDGs largely correspond with states' obligations under international human rights law; specifically the Convention on the Elimination of All Forms of Discrimination Against Women CEDAW (UN 1979) and the International Covenant on Economic, Social, and Cultural Rights (ICESCR) (UN 1966a). Of the 191 UN Member States, 179 have ratified CEDAW and 150 have ratified the ICESCR. The existence of these treaties means that most states have existing, immediate, and binding duties regarding the MDGs. Human rights instruments and mechanisms can potentially be used to mitigate problems caused by the deficiencies of the MDG framework. In turn, the MDGs can potentially mitigate the weaknesses of human rights instruments stemming from lack of political will and vagueness regarding achievable targets. The MDGs need to be achieved if human rights are to be realised.

The GADN believes that understanding and working on the MDGs within a human rights framework can provide activists with tools to challenge inequality and injustice caused by features of the prevailing neo-liberal model of development.[3] This synthesis article, which is an excerpt from a full report (Painter 2004), presents the GADN's perspective on the reviews of the BPFA (UN 1995), the Millennium Declaration (UN GA 2000a), and the MDGs, which will take place in 2005.

Governments have agreed that there should be a formal link between the review of the BPFA and the review of the Millennium Declaration and the MDGs (UN CSW 2004). The 2005 session of the Commission on the Status of Women (CSW) will be a high-level plenary meeting open to UN Member States and Observers, including civil society organisations. They will discuss states' implementation of the BPFA and Beijing+5. The Chairperson of the CSW will then transmit the outcome from this discussion, via the Economic and Social Council of the General Assembly (ECOSOC), to the high-level General Assembly (GA) meeting, which will review the Millennium Declaration in September 2005. This departs from the usual procedure for CSW, in which the annual Agreed Conclusions are considered only by ECOSOC and effectively have no further impact.

The research for this article, which was conducted from June to August 2004 and therefore does not draw on the documents produced by the Millennium Project in January 2005, included desk research and interviews with members of the GADN, staff in the UK Department for International Development (DFID), and staff in the European Commission.

The 2005 reviews

Beijing+10

At the 49th session of the CSW, in March 2005, a review and appraisal will take place of the implementation of the Beijing Declaration, the BPFA, and the outcome of the 23rd special session of the GA in 2000, at which states conducted the first five-year review of the BPFA (UN GA 2000b). Beijing+10 offers opportunities for analysing

progress on women's human rights and holding governments to account. It creates an international space for women to participate in policy debate, to meet each other, to put issues on the agenda, and to lobby their governments. But this opportunity is difficult to realise for many women and women's organisations from the South, because the CSW is held in New York, and costs and visa restrictions make attendance difficult, if not impossible, for many.

The Beijing+10 Review will be conducted by looking at national action plans designed to implement the BPFA, state reports to the committee monitoring CEDAW, information generated through annual CSW sessions, and analysis of questionnaires submitted by states to the UN Division for the Advancement of Women on implementation of the BPFA. Official statistics, Poverty Reduction Strategy Papers (PRSPs), MDG Reports, and other sources of information will also be used. Alongside information about the progress that states have made in implementing the BPFA, reports from Beijing+10 regional preparatory meetings will feed into a final global report.

However, these preparatory meetings have been marked by anti-abortion lobbying and calls to dilute the force of the BPFA text. Some governments have attempted to limit civil society participation in these processes in order to insulate themselves from civil society pressure (Articulación de Mujeres Brasileras *et al.* 2004; APWW 2004). There is a risk that these trends at the preparatory meetings risk will persist and prevail at the Beijing+10 meeting itself.

The Millennium Review

The Millennium Review will be held at a high-level plenary meeting of the UN GA, at the beginning of its 60th session, in New York in September 2005 (UN GA 2004a). The Secretary-General will submit a comprehensive report on the Millennium Declaration (UN GA 2004b, paragraph 5). As the product of the largest-ever gathering of world leaders, the Millennium Declaration sets out a vision for the 21st century. With the exception of a few leakages from other sections, the MDGs come out of the Development and Poverty Eradication section of the Declaration. Thus the Millennium Declaration is broader than the MDGs. The Millennium Review will be informed by the work of the Millennium Project regarding strategies for achieving the MDGs (Sachs and the UN Millennium Project 2005).[4] The 59th GA, currently in session, will be making a final decision on the format and structure of the Millennium Review.

The Millennium Review offers a chance to reaffirm global commitment to achievement of the MDGs. It creates space to stress the importance of a human rights approach to development and to highlight the broader non-discrimination and inclusion agenda that has been overlooked by the MDGs. It is a venue to hold governments to account for their commitments and an opportunity to strengthen advocacy by working in more effective alliances. Given that the 2005 target on girls' education will be missed, the Review could focus attention on the consequences to women, development, and human rights of inadequate concern for gender equality issues.

Despite these hopes, observers are anxious about the global political context, as the rise of fundamentalisms, extremisms, and militarisations has polarised the international community (Barton and Prendergast 2004). Direct civil society participation in the Millennium Review summit in September 2005 itself will not be possible, because of the security concerns and space limitations in the UN building associated with a high-level plenary meeting of the GA (UN GA 2004b, paragraph 21). The Secretary-General has suggested to the Assembly that it organise hearings with civil society organisations prior to the meeting (ibid.). States have already begun their preparations for the Millennium Review. In these national and international processes, there are few opportunities for

experiences from the grassroots to be heard, with particular barriers for women, older people, indigenous people, and poor people. Women's human rights activists are worried that the Millennium Review will overshadow Beijing+10, and there are concerns that women's rights advocates will be running to stand still in the face of better resourced, more organised lobbyists with fundamentalist agendas. Not only are women's human rights under attack: they are also being hijacked, as concepts of gender, equality, and mainstreaming have been turned into symbolic and technical tools to achieve objectives that threaten or ignore women's human rights concerns. It is feared that, as a result of these difficulties, the Millennium Review may not address concerns from activists including the women's movement.

Linking the 2005 reviews

Within the GADN, there is a range of views about how feminist activists should engage, and prioritise, the two reviews of 2005.

Many organisations, from both the North and South, cannot or will not participate in all the global political events and processes around them that are happening in 2005. Some feminist organisations have discussed whether to refuse to engage with the MDG processes (Macdonald 2004). These sentiments flow from a feminist critique of the MDGs and the processes surrounding them, which has exposed the weak integration of gender equality and women's human rights issues. One common critique is that the MDGs are silent on violence against women, and another is that they do not frame reproductive and sexual health as a human rights issue.

The MDGs do not provide a feminist framework for development and human rights. According to the MDGs, the key barriers to women's advancement are high maternal mortality and lack of access for girls to education; but according to the BPFA, there are other barriers in addition to maternal health and girls' education (UN 1995). Women at the Beijing+10 regional preparatory meetings held in 2004 identified a very different set of challenges to gender equality and women's empowerment. These are a weakened women's movement, economic barriers to the empowerment of women, social and cultural attitudes that hinder women's empowerment, problems in 'mainstreaming' (integrating) gender issues into governance and development, and an adverse international economic environment. Only one Beijing+10 report cited high maternal mortality and lack of girls' access to education as top priority (UN Economic Commission for Africa 2004). Obviously, this does not mean that maternal mortality and girls' education are irrelevant for women's human rights. Rather, it shows that using the BPFA as a framework reveals different priorities from those identified in the MDGs – priorities that go to the core of the fundamental and structural roots of women's human rights violations.

There are further concerns among feminist activists that the MDG framework is distracting governments from their obligations under international human rights treaties, and the Millennium Review process is overshadowing other monitoring and accountability mechanisms (Obando 2003). These concerns are discussed in more detail in the section that follows. Some advocates fear that linking the reviews will result in the marginalisation of the BPFA. One major effect of this would be that women's human rights in developed countries would receive no attention, because the Millennium Review and the MDGs are understood as relevant only for developing countries, while the international human rights obligations under CEDAW and commitments under Beijing apply in all countries.

Women's human rights advocates should consider these issues in shaping their strategies for engagement. Yet, despite these concerns, many feminist activists see it as essential to engage with the MDG process. The GADN has decided that the opportunity to link the Millennium Review and the Beijing+10 Review needs to be taken up. We need to emphasise the importance of gender equality and gender mainstreaming if the MDGs are to be achieved. The Millennium Review offers us a chance to put issues of importance to women on the MDG agenda. In addition, engagement with the MDG process presents us with an opportunity to challenge the development model that is being promoted to achieve the MDGs, and to stress that global economic justice, peaceful resolution of international disputes, and sustainability are essential for achievement of the MDGs (Barton 2004).

Linkages in policy-making

The MDGs originated in the Millennium Declaration, which, in turn, has its roots in the Platforms for Action agreed at the series of global conferences held in the 1990s. These were founded on international human rights treaties, including the International Covenant on Civil and Political Rights (ICCPR), the ICESCR, and CEDAW.

Yet despite their origins in human rights, the MDGs are being used in support of a neo-liberal model of development, which we believe threatens the realisation of human rights and gender equality. Many international agencies and donors have committed themselves to the MDGs. But these commitments are not worth much if they do not address the incoherence that results from pursuing the MDGs while continuing to follow a development model that equates economic growth with human development. For example, women's empowerment is pursued in the MDGs because it has high 'payoffs' for economic growth and poverty reduction: studies have shown that a failure to meet the goal of gender equality in education will lead to economic growth losses (Abu-Ghaida and Klasen 2003).

In fact, attaining the MDGs means shaking the pillars of the growth-driven model of development. The MDGs require investments in health, education, and infrastructure (Vandemoortele 2004), while the neo-liberal model emphasises a reduction in state expenditure for purposes of financial stability (Dollar and Kraay 2002). A major reason for failure to meet the MDGs thus far is that governments and donors are failing to invest in services, failing to take advantage of cross-sectoral synergies, and failing to foster an enabling international environment (Vandemoortele 2003).

Advocates can use the human rights obligations of states to challenge policy decisions taken by governments in the name of reaching the MDGs, if these violate human rights. International human rights treaties, such as the ICESCR, the ICCPR, and CEDAW, create a minimum standard for national legislation and policy making. They define what governments agreed they must achieve.

The ICESCR and the ICCPR establish that states must not discriminate (Article 2 of each), and must guarantee the equal rights of women and men to the enjoyment of rights (Article 3 of each). Under the ICESCR, states have obligations to take progressive steps towards achieving the full realisation of economic, social, and cultural rights, using all appropriate means including the adoption of legislative measures (Article 2). The concept of progressive realisation captures the idea that achievement of these rights will not happen overnight, but instead requires gradual progress over time. Signatories to the ICESCR are obliged to take immediate, deliberate, concrete, and targeted steps towards the full realisation of the rights set out in the ICESCR, within a reasonably short time of ratification. No matter how a state is doing on progressively realising the rights to health, or education, or work, it has an immediate obligation to do so in a non-discriminatory way (Aurora *et al.* 2002).

CEDAW strengthens the non-discrimination provisions in the ICCPR and ICESCR by defining and protecting the human rights of women specifically. States that are party to CEDAW must prohibit discrimination against women in their laws, as well as in the practice of public authorities and institutions, and they must pursue a national policy to eliminate such discrimination (Article 2). Under CEDAW, states must take all appropriate measures to ensure the full development and advancement of women (Article 3), and to address the structural, social, and cultural patterns that underpin discrimination against women (Article 5). Under CEDAW, states have an immediate obligation to pursue a policy of eliminating discrimination (Article 2). Yet the majority of the provisions in CEDAW are phrased as obligations to take all appropriate measures, because these rights must be progressively realised over time. Thus, the obligation to make policies that will help get the result is immediate, while the obligation to actually attain the result is gradual.

The ICESCR deals with this difference between obligations of conduct and obligations of result with the concept of progressive realisation. To ensure that progressive realisation is not used to argue that states can meet their obligations just by enacting policies, the concept of minimum core obligations has been developed to define a limited sphere of obligations of result (Committee on Economic, Social and Cultural Rights 1990). These define the rock-bottom responsibilities of states in terms of economic, social, and cultural rights. A state is presumed to have failed in its ICESCR obligations if significant numbers of its population are deprived of the right to food, the right to essential primary health care, the right to basic shelter and housing, or the right to the most basic forms of education (ibid.). The Committee monitoring the ICESCR has further defined and articulated these core obligations in a number of General Comments on housing (Committee on Economic, Social and Cultural Rights 1991), food (Committee on Economic, Social and Cultural Rights 1999c), education (Committee on Economic, Social and Cultural Rights 1999a, 1999b), health (Committee on Economic, Social and Cultural Rights 2000), and water (Committee on Economic, Social and Cultural Rights 2002).

States are obliged to take steps towards the realisation of these rights as far as their resources allow them to. Resources are defined as coming from within the state, and also as a result of international co-operation. For that reason, they say nothing regarding the roles of the public and private sectors in provision (Hunt 2004).

The MDGs have been described as 'minimum development goals'. This mirrors the human rights concept of core obligations. States' core obligations roughly correspond to the MDGs. The MDGs and human rights are interconnected and indivisible. Table 1 shows only the most obvious links and intersections.

Using human rights instruments helps to expose the fact that states are already under the following obligations:

- *Non-discrimination*: All steps taken towards achievement of the MDGs should benefit people equally and in a non-discriminatory way. An obligation to mainstream or integrate gender inequality in the MDGs can be grounded in the immediate obligation of state signatories to CEDAW to pursue a policy of eliminating discrimination against women (Article 2). CEDAW (Article 2) obligates states to mainstream or integrate a commitment to gender equality within each Goal (Waldorf 2004). Activists can use the BPFA to advocate that the international community has reached a common understanding of the definition of gender mainstreaming and its requirements.[5]

- *Non-infringement*: In order to attain the MDGs, states may not infringe people's enjoyment and exercise of their rights.

- *Non-retrogression*: In order to attain the MDGs, states need to ensure that rights that have previously been realised are not curtailed. States may not reverse

Table 1: Interconnections between the MDGs and human rights

Goals and targets from the Millennium Declaration	Core obligations under the ICESCR
Goal 1: Eradicate extreme poverty and hunger	Basic housing Adequate food
Goal 2: Achieve universal primary education	Basic education
Goal 3: Promote gender equality and empower women	Basic education Primary health care
Goal 4: Reduce child mortality	Adequate food Primary health care Water
Goal 5: Improve maternal health	Adequate food Primary health care Water
Goal 6: Combat HIV/AIDS, malaria, and other diseases	Primary health care Water
Goal 7: Ensure environmental sustainability	Basic housing Water

legislation that has already resulted in rights being realised (for example by criminalising abortion where it has been legalised, or by introducing user fees for primary education).

- *Progressive realisation*: States have a legal obligation to work progressively towards achievement of the MDGs, because realisation of human rights requires achievement of the Goals.

- *Realisation of core obligations*: The fact that states are under the core obligations mentioned earlier of basic housing, adequate food, basic education, primary health care (including maternal health), and water can be used in MDG processes to argue for the prioritisation of government actions to meet core obligations over other potential actions (for example research into new weapons).

Using these principles, the ICESCR, CEDAW, and the BPFA can be used as advocacy tools to lend authority to specific policy recommendations for the realisation of human rights, thus helping to challenge inequality-enhancing, growth-driven development interventions.

Building the links among the ICESCR, CEDAW, the BPFA, and the MDGs in this way shows that the MDGs are not lofty global commitments being pursued out of global charity. They are actually concrete human rights obligations, which must be prioritised and achieved in a non-discriminatory way. Reframing the MDGs as human rights obligations changes the debate from the language of will and commitment to the language of duty and obligation.

Analysis and monitoring

However, a shortcoming of these human rights instruments is that they fail to define how rights should be realised, and what states are obligated to do. In its General Comments, the Committee monitoring the ICESCR has sought to define the nature of states' obligations to ensure rights, including

those relating to health and education. Although these documents give greater clarity, their existence demonstrates that the ICESCR lacks specific goals and targets for effective monitoring of government progress. The BPFA also suffers from a lack of clear indicators to assess governments' performance against their commitments (Timothy and Freeman 2000).

The GADN believes that using human rights instruments can improve monitoring of the MDGs, in terms of what is being measured and how the information is being analysed. A human rights approach encourages disaggregation of data, a broader definition of poverty, and analysis of causes and consequences.

The MDG targets and indicators are widely acclaimed as representing an international consensus on global development goals. With their measurable targets and indicators, the MDGs should be less vague than human rights instruments about the nature of progress to be realised. They could potentially help states to measure their progress in attaining human rights. However, this would be possible only by addressing questions about what is measured in the MDGs and how progress is monitored. These problems make the MDGs and their indicators unreliable yardsticks of progress (Vandemoortele 2004).

The indicators used to measure achievement of the MDGs risk generating problems. If the narrow aims of achieving numerical goals drive policy-making decisions, the policies would only be as good as the goals and indicators being measured. For example, the use of World Bank indexes to measure poverty under Goal 1 of the MDGs of poverty results in an under-estimation of poverty, due in part to reliance on national household surveys which mask inequality among different individuals and categories of people within households, and fail to disaggregate between data from rural and urban areas (ibid.). Reliance on this kind of averaged and aggregated data means that it would be possible, in statistical terms, to achieve the MDGs globally by ensuring progress on indicators in the most populous countries and ignoring sparsely populated countries, regions within countries, groups within societies, or individuals within households in which poverty would remain unaddressed.

There are crucial flaws in the method for monitoring progress on the MDGs. Mechanisms for monitoring progress on the MDGs currently include annual UN global reports, five-year comprehensive reviews, and country-level MDG Reports. A UNDP evaluation revealed serious problems with the MDG Reports. These problems concerned the need for sex-disaggregated data, national participation and ownership, synergies with other reporting processes, and capacity (UNDP 2003). There is insufficient scope in the MDG Reports for analysis of why progress has or has not been achieved, and no mechanism to explore the impact of factors that fall beyond the scope of the MDGs (like peace and security). Furthermore, a recent gender evaluation of the MDG Reports showed dismal performance in integrating gender analysis into the issues, or attention to women's empowerment (Menon-Sen 2003). Women are seen as vulnerable victims and mothers, rather than as agents of development.

These problems notwithstanding, there is some evidence at a country level of progress being made in more effective and gender-sensitive monitoring. In Viet Nam and Cambodia, the indicators and targets have been made more context-specific, to recognise that the global targets may be inadequate (for example because they are unattainable or have already been reached). The Cambodian Country Report had strong emphasis on ensuring that the statistics used for the indicators are disaggregated by sex (Hyun n.d.). The Albanian government has brought the MDGs down to a sub-national level by developing regional MDG Reports, and it has identified gender mainstreaming

as one of its approaches to the MDGs.

Advocates can use states' obligations under human rights treaties to challenge the problems surrounding what is measured and how progress is monitored to achieve the MDGs. The principle of equality and non-discrimination (found in the UN Charter (Articles 1, 2 and 7), the ICCPR (Article 26), the ICESCR (Articles 2 and 3), the Convention on the Elimination of All Forms of Racial Discrimination (CERD; UN 1969), and CEDAW) puts signatory states under an immediate obligation of non-discrimination. These obligations mean that states should not claim achievement of a Goal if, in the process, inequality has been perpetuated or exacerbated. A commitment to non-discrimination and equality requires specific attention to groups that experience discrimination or disadvantage. This requires states to look for evidence about the impact of policies on different social groups. Thus, advocates can argue that measuring progress on achievement of the MDGs using only averages and aggregates violates that obligation of non-discrimination.

A human rights approach regards development and poverty alleviation as processes towards the realisation of human rights. Further, a feminist human rights approach to development requires more than just identifying that women are an adversely affected group, but analysing why (Dairiam 2002). The MDGs describe symptoms of poverty, rather than analysing causes.

The understanding of poverty in the MDGs demonstrates this problem. The MDGs, in particular Goal 1, understand poverty narrowly in terms of economic want, and fail to take account of social and political marginalisation, which is both an outcome and a primary cause of poverty. The definition of poverty does not consider why and how women's experience of poverty differs from that of men. An holistic definition of poverty would address the need to attain the goals of human security (encompassing security from gender-based violence, to security from armed conflict), reproductive and sexual rights, and sustainable development. These social and political dimensions of poverty are currently addressed under other MDGs, or not addressed at all, yet they are intrinsically linked to what is defined and isolated in Goal 1 as 'poverty'. Without considering the social and political dimensions of poverty, the analysis that shapes anti-poverty policies aimed at reaching Goal 1 misses the nature of the problems facing women.

Activists can use the human rights framework to strengthen arguments for more holistic definitions of poverty. The idea that human rights are indivisible leads to the conclusion that tackling poverty requires understanding and addressing the interlocking and interdependent causes of poverty, rather than focusing narrowly on one aspect of poverty, such as economic want. CEDAW can help activists to ask and answer questions about who is affected by poverty, and why. Its definition of discrimination (Article 1) covers any distinction, exclusion, or restriction that has the purpose or effect of being discriminatory against women, thus including both *de jure* and *de facto* equality (Byrnes 2002). Using CEDAW's definition of discrimination directs attention towards the root causes of discrimination against women, not just factual descriptions of gender inequality.

CEDAW offers additional arguments for the activist's toolbox

CEDAW bridges the traditional division between civil and political rights, and economic, social, and cultural rights and reaffirms the indivisibility of human rights (Dairiam 2002). CEDAW affirms not only women's equal rights to participate in public political decision-making, but also their equal rights within the family (Article 16), in a shift from other human rights instruments that designate the family as a unit to be protected from state interference (Byrnes 2002). General Recommendations of the CEDAW Committee, General Comments from the ICESCR Committee, and the BPFA can be used to analyse discrimination against women to determine its causes and consequences.

Accountability

Linking the MDGs to international human rights in feminist advocacy work brings human rights accountability mechanisms into the MDG process. In addition to changing the terms of accountability from commitment to obligation, this brings the benefits of an institutionalised process and an established role for civil society.

Weak accountability mechanisms accompany the MDGs, because the Millennium Declaration is a non-binding political declaration, and the MDGs are goals, not obligations. The MDG Reports are not linked up to states' existing reporting obligations under human rights treaties. There is no established procedure for civil society to participate in the MDG reporting process or to submit alternative reports. The most obvious vacuum in accountability surrounds Goal 8 on aid. In contrast to the seven other MDGs, there are no time-frames, quantifiable benchmarks, or instruments to monitor rich countries, financial institutions, and corporations. There are a few countries that are voluntarily producing their own reports on progress towards Goal 8. But the lack of global monitoring of Goal 8 shows that developing countries are being held to account for their successes and failures in overcoming enormous human development challenges, whereas rich countries have no reporting obligations (Birdsall and Clemens 2003).

Human rights machineries, such as those available through CEDAW, the ICESCR, and the BPFA, could be used to challenge these weaknesses in accountability by arguing that not only are states politically committed to the MDGs, they are also legally obligated as parties to human rights treaties (Center for Human Rights and Global Justice 2003). This would create scope for linking the MDGs to reporting processes under human rights treaties, and provide more space for NGOs to engage in the process.

Parties to CEDAW submit regular reports to the Committee on the Elimination of Discrimination Against Women on the measures they have taken to give effect to the provisions of the treaty. Civil society organisations may submit alternative Shadow Reports on progress in their country. The Committee reviews these reports and offers suggestions and recommendations. A similar process exists under the ICESCR.

There are weaknesses in the reporting processes: the Committees have backlogs of states' reports, and some countries do not submit reports (Flinterman 2004). In contrast to CEDAW, there is no state-by-state review of progress in implementing the BPFA. There are global-level review processes, but they produce conclusions that do not translate easily into practical recommendations at a national level. Furthermore, some states use these global-level reviews as an opportunity to seek to renegotiate the text of the BPFA.

Despite their problems, CEDAW, the ICESCR, and the BPFA offer a framework for holding governments to account for their obligations on human rights. CEDAW and the ICESCR offer the advantage of specific state-by-state reports, while the BPFA brings a global process that is more likely to generate global political interest. CEDAW, the ICESCR, and the BPFA offer established processes for civil society organisations to participate and hold their governments to account. The BPFA helps to guide advocacy work, because the Critical Areas of Concern direct attention to areas where governments are failing to keep their promises. GADN members, like many other civil society organisations, have experience of using these human rights instruments to remind governments of their obligations.

However, the issues around the lack of accountability regarding Goal 8 do not seem easily solved by reference to human rights instruments, because there is little consensus on the right to development as an enforceable human right.

Participation

The MDGs emerged in the context of a development approach that emphasises the importance of participation, grassroots engagement, and empowerment. But many civil society organisations from the North and South feel they were not involved in the establishment of the MDGs; thus, ownership of the process is weak (Bissio 2003). The recent establishment of the Millennium Campaign aimed at harnessing civil society support signals an acknowledgement by the international community of this problem. Urban, middle-class, advocacy-oriented organisations tend to be over-represented in international human rights activism, while small, grassroots organisations face major barriers to effective participation in these processes. The GADN and others must work to overcome these inequalities by promoting participation and partnership at grassroots and international levels (Hayes 2004).

Weak civil society participation in the MDG process, both at national and international levels, is not only a threat to the achievement of the MDGs. It is also contrary to the right to take part in the conduct of public affairs, which is protected under the ICCPR (Article 25), and the right under CEDAW to participate in the formulation of government policy (Article 7). Activists can use the ICCPR and CEDAW to argue that they have rights to participate in the MDG process. This means being part of the policy-making process, nationally and internationally, as well as the national and global reviews.

In addition to grounding the claim for participation, human rights instruments also ground the practical experience of participation, because human rights advocacy has been a key stronghold for civil society. CEDAW has been invoked in support of efforts to enact or amend laws (McPhedran 2000). The experience of being involved in advocacy around the UN World Conferences, such as the 1995 Beijing Conference, has developed advocacy skills in women's NGOs, raised the profile of international human rights instruments as tools for the promotion of gender equality, and helped to put women's organisations on the map as legitimate watchdogs of government action (Timothy and Freeman 2000).

Using human rights instruments and processes can facilitate genuine partnerships between civil society in the North and South, because all societies have yet to realise the promise of human rights. The BPFA and CEDAW address gender inequality and women's human rights in all countries, North and South, poor and rich, and represent a shared agenda among women's organisations working in different contexts. This can counter the concern that the MDGs focus on developing countries and ignore development challenges in rich countries.

In these ways, the processes surrounding the ICESCR, CEDAW, and the BPFA can help to fill the participation deficit in the MDGs.

Political will

The Millennium Declaration and the MDGs have captured political attention, helped to revitalise international aid flows, and focused attention at an institutional level on targets (Barton 2004). The MDGs receive more attention than human rights, particularly as commitments to international human rights and humanitarian law treaties are rescinded by some states. Lack of political will is the fatal flaw for the ICESCR, the BPFA, CEDAW, and many international human rights mechanisms. The BPFA is particularly vulnerable, because of its status as the outcome of a conference rather than a treaty. There are few states that view the women's human rights agenda as a high priority issue, and a handful openly obstruct it. Building linkages between MDGs and human rights instruments can benefit women's human rights activism by harnessing global political will.

The lack of consensus around the concept of a 'right to development' means that human rights instruments do not bring much to the creation of a concrete obligation of international co-operation between rich and poor states (Piron 2002). The MDGs go some way to address this problem. Goal 8, despite its weaknesses, provides a framework for calling for improved international aid and co-operation. This approach could be stronger than the human rights route because the international community has agreed to this Global Partnership for Development.

In order to bring these various strands together, I offer an example which shows, in practice, what can be achieved by linking the MDGs and human rights.[6] As part of the CEDAW reporting process in Nepal, Women for Human Rights (WHR) and Single Women's Group (SWG) submitted a Shadow Report to the Committee on breaches of their government's treaty obligations in relation to widows. Subsequently, the UNDP raised the issue of the situation of widows with the government, in the context of the MDGs. The government has since asked WHR to conduct a situational analysis of widows' lives in the context of human rights and the MDGs. WHR and SWG are using the CEDAW Committee's Concluding Comments and their ongoing research to support their lobbying efforts.

Through strategic advocacy work using human rights instruments and processes, WHR and SWG have made the government and donor community 'see' a social group that had been marginalised. CEDAW's definition of discrimination helped to expose widows' particular experiences of inequality, and the reporting process offered the NGOs a chance to hold their government to account. The UNDP became involved through its commitment to meeting the MDGs. Thus, activists in Nepal have reaped the rewards of the MDGs and human rights processes: CEDAW offered a framework for analysing discrimination, a formal accountability process, and established routes for NGO participation; and the MDGs opened up space for dialogue between governments and donors and helped to generate political will. The crucial spark was the CEDAW Shadow Report, but nothing would have caught light without the work of strong and strategic women's human rights activists. Thus, the experience in Nepal exemplifies the synergies and rewards that can be found in linking human rights to the MDGs.

Conclusion

Women's human rights activists should recognise the Millennium Review for the global political momentum that it is generating. The task is to help to ensure that this momentum is directed towards achievement of human rights. To that end, the GADN aims to be one of the organisations acting as a bridge between the Millennium Review and the Beijing+10 Review, by focusing on both Reviews in its advocacy activities.

Activists in support of women's human rights should argue from the standpoint that the MDGs correspond with states' core obligations under international human rights treaties. States that are parties to the ICESCR and CEDAW have existing, immediate, and binding obligations to work progressively towards achievement of the MDGs, in ways that neither intend, nor result in, gender-based discrimination.

By building a complementary relationship between the MDGs and human rights, human rights can act as a check on neo-liberal strategies to achieve the MDGs. Human rights treaties and processes bring the force of obligation, and the MDGs bring the power of motivation, to ensure that states move from commitments to action. Together, they can help to realise the promise of the Millennium Declaration and the Universal Declaration of Human Rights.

Genevieve Renard Painter works on gender, development, and human rights issues and is currently pursuing a law degree with a focus on human rights. The author thanks Nicola Painter and those who gave their time for extensive interviews. She can be reached at genevievepainter@yahoo.com.

Notes

1 The UK Gender and Development Network (GADN) is a diverse membership network of 200 representatives of development organisations and individuals, working to promote gender equality and gender mainstreaming in development in the UK. This GADN project was made possible through the support of the Department for International Development.

2 The GADN aims to strengthen members' work by keeping them informed of gender and development issues through networking, information sharing, and the commissioning of quality research. The GADN acts as an effective advocacy tool for gender and development concerns by working closely with government and other decision-making bodies. While this article stems from broad consultation with the GADN membership, it does not necessarily reflect the views of all its members. For more information about the Network, please contact gadnetwork@womankind.org.uk.

3 However, it acknowledges that other strategies linking the MDGs and human rights may be more appropriate within other contexts.

4 The Millennium Project is an independent adviser to the UN Secretary-General and is composed of Task Forces related to the MDGs. The Task Forces are made up of independent scholars, staff from the UN agencies, and other public, non-government, and private-sector institutions. The work of the Task Forces has fed into the Millennium Project's Final Synthesis report (Sachs and UN Millennium Project 2005).

5 The BPFA states that 'Governments and other actors should promote an active and visible policy of mainstreaming a gender perspective in all policies and programmes so that, before decisions are taken, an analysis is made of the effects on women and men, respectively' (paragraph 202). The strategic objectives under this section include creating or strengthening

national machineries (paragraph 203), integrating a gender perspective in legislation, public policies, programmes, and projects (paragraphs 204–5), and generating and disseminating gender-disaggregated data and information for planning and evaluation (paragraphs 206–9).

6 This example draws on a presentation by Lily Thapa (2004). For more information, contact Lily Thapa at WHR (lily@mos.com.np) or Margaret Owen at Widows for Peace through Democracy (margieowen@aol.com).

References

Abu-Ghaida, D. and S. Klasen (2003) 'The Costs of Missing the Millennium Development Goal on Gender Equity', Discussion Paper, University of Munich, Department of Economics, papers.ssrn.com/sol3/papers.cfm?abstract_id=5 15945 (checked February 2005)

APWW (2004) 'Statement of the Asia Pacific NGO Forum on Beijing +10', www.hrea.org/lists/hre-asiapacific/markup/msg00116.html (checked February 2005)

Articulación de Mujeres Brasileras *et al.* (2004) 'Novena Conferencia Regional sobre la Mujer de América Latina y el Caribe: Declaración de Organizaciones de la Sociedad Civil', Mexico City: Comisión Económica para América Latina y el Caribe

Aurora, S. *et al.* (2002) 'Montréal Principles on Women's Economic, Social and Cultural Rights', Project of Women's Working Group of the International Network for Economic, Social and Cultural Rights, www.escr-net.org/ WorkingGroupDocs/MontrealPrinciples.doc (checked February 2005)

Barton, C. (2004) Presentation reported in M. Macdonald (ed.) (2004)

Barton, C. and L. Prendergast (eds.) (2004) 'Seeking Accountability on Women's Human Rights: Women Debate the UN Millennium Development Goals', New York: Women's International Coalition for Economic Justice

Birdsall, N. and M. Clemens (2003) 'From Promise to Performance: How Rich Countries Can Help Poor Countries Help Themselves', Washington DC: Center for Global Development Brief 2(1)

Bissio, R. (2003) 'Civil society and the MDGs', *Development Policy Journal* 3, April: 151–60

Byrnes, A. (2002) 'The Convention on the Elimination of All Forms of Discrimination Against Women', in W. Benedek (ed.) *The Human Rights of Women: International Instruments and African Experiences*, London: Zed Books

Center for Human Rights and Global Justice (2003) 'Human Rights Perspectives on the Millennium Development Goals: Conference Report', New York: NYU School of Law

Committee on Economic, Social and Cultural Rights (1990) 'General Comment on the Nature of States Parties' Obligations (Art. 2, Para. 1)', report on the Fourth and Fifth Sessions, UN ESCOR (Official Records of the Economic and Social Council), 1991, Supp. No. 2, UN Doc. E/1991/23 E/C.12/1990/8

Committee on Economic, Social and Cultural Rights (1991) 'General Comment on the Right to Adequate Housing (Art. 11, Para. 1)', report on the Sixth and Seventh Sessions, UN ESCOR (Official Records of the Economic and Social Council), 1992, Supp. No. 2, UN Doc E/1992/23 E/C.12/1991/4

Committee on Economic, Social and Cultural Rights (1999a) 'General Comment on Plans of Action for Primary Education (Art. 14)', report on the Twentieth and Twenty-first Sessions, UN ESCOR (Official Records of the Economic and Social Council), 2000, Supp. No. 2, UN Doc. E/2000/22 E/C.12/1999/11

Committee on Economic, Social and Cultural Rights (1999b) 'General Comment on the Right to Education (Art. 13)', report on the Twentieth and Twenty-first Sessions, UN ESCOR (Official Records of the Economic and Social Council), 2000, Supp. No. 2, UN Doc. E/2000/22 E/C.12/1999/11

Committee on Economic, Social and Cultural Rights (1999c) 'General Comment on the Right to Adequate Food (Art. 11)', report on the Twentieth and Twenty-first Sessions, UN ESCOR (Official Records of the Economic and Social Council), 2000, Supp. No. 2, UN Doc. E/2000/22 E/C.12/1999/11

Committee on Economic, Social and Cultural Rights (2000) 'General Comment on the Right to the Highest Attainable Standard of Health (Art. 12)', report on the Twenty-second, Twenty-third, and Twenty-fourth Sessions, UN ESCOR (Official Records of the Economic and Social Council), 2001, Supp. No. 2, UN. Doc. E/2001/22 E/C.12/2000/21

Committee on Economic, Social and Cultural Rights (2002) 'General Comment on the Right to Water (Arts. 11 and 12)', report on the Twenty-eighth and Twenty-ninth Sessions, UN ESCOR (Official Records of the Economic and Social Council), 2003, Supp. No. 2, UN Doc. E/2003/22 E/C.12/2002/13

Dairiam, S. (2002) 'The Areas of Common Grounds Among Various UN Guiding Instruments – CEDAW, Beijing Platform for Action, and the Outcomes Document', presented at the Expert Group Meeting on Regional Implementation and Monitoring of the Beijing Platform for Action and the Outcome of the 23rd Special Session of the UN General Assembly Relating to Women, International Women's Rights Action Watch Asia Pacific, www.iwraw-ap.org/aboutus/paper07.htm (checked February 2005)

Dollar, D. and A. Kraay (2002) 'Growth is good for the poor', *Journal of Economic Growth* 7(3): 195–225

Flinterman, C. (2004) 'UN Treaty-based Mechanisms: CEDAW', presentation given at the International Human Rights Academy, Utrecht, 15–28 August 2004

Hayes, C. (2004) 'Out of the Margins: An Analysis of the Millennium Development Goals from a Women's Human Rights Perspective', London: WOMANKIND Worldwide

Hunt, P. (2004) 'UN Special Rapporteur: Reporting and Effects', presentation given at the International Human Rights Academy, Utrecht, 15–28 August 2004

Hyun, M. (n.d.) 'Project Narrative Report. Engendering the Cambodia Country Report for the Millennium Development Goals (MDGs)', UNIFEM-UNDP SPPD CMB/02/018/77, www.mdgender.net/resources/monograph_detail.php?MonographID=23 (checked February 2005)

Macdonald, M. (ed.) (2004) 'A Report of WIDE's Annual Conference. Globalising Women's Rights: Confronting Unequal Development Between the UN Rights Framework and the WTO Trade Agreements', Brussels: Women in Development Europe

McPhedran, M. (2000) *The First CEDAW Impact Study: Final Report*, Toronto: Centre for Feminist Research and The International Women's Rights Project, York University

Menon-Sen, K. (2003) 'Millennium Development Goals. National Reports: A Look Through a Gender Lens', New York: UNDP

Obando, A.E. (2003) 'Women and the Millennium Development Goals',

www.whrnet.org/docs/issue-mdg.html (last checked by the author February 2005)

Painter, G. (2004) 'Gender, the Millennium Development Goals, and Human Rights in the Context of the 2005 Review Processes', London: GADN

Piron, L. (2002) 'The Right to Development: A Review of the Current State of the Debate for the Department for International Development', London: Overseas Development Institute

Sachs, J.D. and the UN Millennium Project (2005) *Investing in Development: A Practical Plan to Achieve the Millennium Development Goals*, London: Earthscan

Thapa, L. (2004) 'Impacts of Conflict on Widows of Nepal', paper presented at the conference on Global Challenges to Women's Rights: 25 Years of CEDAW, London, 9 December 2004

Timothy, K. and M. Freeman (2000) 'The CEDAW Convention and the Beijing Platform for Action: Reinforcing the Promise of the Rights Framework', iwraw.igc.org/beijing5/freeman-timothy-paper.htm (last checked by the author February 2005)

UN (1966a) *Covenant on Economic, Social and Cultural Rights*, 993 UNTS 3

UN (1966b) *Covenant on Civil and Political Rights*, 999 UNTS 171

UN (1969) *International Convention on the Elimination of All Forms of Racial Discrimination*, 660 UNTS

UN (1979) 'Convention on the Elimination of All Forms of Discrimination Against Women', 1249 UNTS 13, www.un.org/womenwatch/daw/cedaw/ (checked March 2005)

UN (1995) *Report of the Fourth World Conference on Women, Beijing, 4–15 September 1995*, Sales No. E.96.IV.13, New York: United Nations Publications

UN CSW (2004) 'Report on the Forty-eighth Session, 1–12 March 2004', UN ESCOR (Official Records of the Economic and Social Council), 2004, Supp. No. 7, UN Doc. E/2004/27-E/CN.6/2004/14

UNDP (2003) 'Millennium Development Goals Reports: An Assessment', New York: UNDP

UN Economic Commission for Africa (2004) 'Report of the Sub-regional Decade Review Meeting on the Implementation of the Beijing Platform for Action in Eastern Africa', 2–4 June 2004, www.uneca.org/beijingplus10/East%20africa%20draft%20report-English.pdf (checked February 2005)

UN GA (2000a) 'Millennium Declaration', GA Res. 55/2, UN GAOR (General Assembly Official Records), Fifty-fifth Session, UN Doc. A/Res/55/2

UN GA (2000b) 'Further Actions and Initiatives to Implement the Beijing Declaration and Platform for Action', GA Res. S-23/3, UN GAOR (General Assembly Official Records), Twenty-third Special Session, UN Doc. A/Res/S-23/3

UN GA (2004a) 'Follow-up to the Outcome of the Millennium Summit and Integrated and Coordinated Implementation of and Follow-up to the Outcomes of the Major United Nations Conferences and Summits in the Economic and Social Fields', GA Res. 58/291, UN GAOR (General Assembly Official Records), Fifty-eighth Session, UN Doc. A/Res/58/291

UN GA (2004b) 'Modalities, Format and Organization of the High-level Plenary Meeting of the Sixtieth Session of the General Assembly: Report of the Secretary-General', UN GAOR (General Assembly Official Records), Fifty-ninth Session, UN Doc. A/59/545

Vandemoortele, J. (2003) 'Are the MDGs feasible?', *Development Policy Journal* 3, April: 1–22

Vandemoortele, J. (2004) 'Can the MDGs Foster a New Partnership for Pro-poor Policies?', New York: UNDP

Waldorf, L. (2004) 'Pathway to Gender Equality: CEDAW, Beijing, and the MDGs', New York: UN Development Fund for Women and Berlin: GTZ

Critiquing the MDGs from a Caribbean perspective[1]

Peggy Antrobus

This article explores ways in which the MDGs can be made to work to promote women's equality and empowerment. Drawn from the author's extensive experience of feminist activism in the Caribbean region, it discusses strategies to improve the MDGs.

Overall, as a feminist I think of the MDGs as a Major Distraction Gimmick – a distraction from the much more important Platforms for Action from the UN conferences of the 1990s, in Rio 1992 (Environment), Vienna 1993 (Human Rights), Cairo 1994 (Population), Copenhagen (Social Development) and Beijing 1995 (Women), Istanbul 1996 (Habitats), and Rome 1997 (Food), on which the MDGs are based. But despite believing this, I think it worthwhile to join other activists within women's movements who are currently developing strategies to try to ensure that the MDGs can be made to work to promote women's equality and empowerment.

This article is written in response to the need to do this. It draws on my experience of working in this field for more than 30 years, and makes particular reference to Caribbean women's realities. First, I worked within the bureaucracy as Director of the Jamaican Women's Bureau. Second, I was head of what used to be the University of the West Indies' (UWI's) major outreach programme for women, the Women and Development Unit (WAND), where, in 1981, we tested a pilot project aimed at promoting women's

empowerment. Third, I am a feminist activist who is involved in the global women's movement as part of the DAWN network. Finally, I did doctoral research on the links between global trends, development strategies (including the macro-economic policy framework of structural adjustment), the impacts on poor women, and possible interventions aimed at achieving the goal of women's equality and empowerment, and all that goes with that.

What can be said in favour of the MDGs? As the United Nations Development Fund for Women (UNIFEM) and many others point out, when viewed within the context of the new aid agenda, the MDGs provide a common framework, agreed to by all governments. They have measurable targets and indicators of progress, around which governments, UN agencies, international financial institutions, and civil society alike can rally. They provide a 'strategic talking point for assessing what the barriers to the achievement of goals are, and provide a tool with which to hold both donor agencies and governments accountable' (White 2001, 2002, cited by Subrahmanian 2003, 3). Goal 3, on gender equality and the empowerment of women, has been argued by some to be 'symbolic of the significant impact of feminist advocacy over years in making the case for gender-aware development' (Subrahmanian 2003, 1), despite the fact that we know the emptiness of rhetorical statements on gender.

On the other hand, there is widespread awareness of the limitations of the MDGs as an approach. First, to treat each Goal as separate ignores the ways in which they are interconnected. In relation to the empowerment of women specifically, this limitation is particularly challenging because of the complex relationships between women's equality and empowerment – Goal 3 – and all the other Goals. As the International Center for Research on Women Report notes (ICRW 2003), none of the other MDGs can be achieved without the achievement of women's equality and empowerment. The other goals and targets – eradicating extreme poverty and hunger (Goal 1); achieving universal primary education (Goal 2); reducing child mortality (Goal 4); improving maternal health (Goal 5); combating HIV/AIDS, malaria, and other diseases (Goal 6); and ensuring environmental sustainability (Goal 7, including Target 10, access to safe water) – are all related in some significant way to the position of women and to the conditions under which they live in any society.

For women, the Beijing Platform for Action remains the most important basic text. Structured around 12 Priority Areas of Concern, its theoretical framework is consistent and much more comprehensive. It addresses gender issues from within a theoretical framework of social reproduction, which relates to the realities of women's lives and the ways in which women organise, and considers each of the Priority Areas in relation to women's equality and empowerment. The Priority Areas are: 1 Poverty; 2 Education and Training; 3 Access to Health Care and Related Services; 4 The Elimination of Violence Against Women; 5

Women Living in Situations of Conflict and Under Foreign Occupation; 6 Economic Structures and Policies; 7 Sharing of Power and Decision-Making; 8 Mechanisms for the Advancement of Women; 9 Human Rights; 10 Access to Communications Systems; 11 Management of Natural Resources; 12 Rights of the Girl Child.

For women, the MDGs have inadequate targets and indicators. The indicators used are restricted to quantifiable indicators, when much of what is most important – such as women's equality and empowerment – is not easily quantifiable. In addition, they omit important goals and targets, such as the elimination of violence against women and sexual and reproductive rights.

The political economy of the MDGs

From the perspective of women, the political economy of the MDGs is one dominated by the twin demons of religious and economic fundamentalism.

I first heard of the MDGs through the outraged response of the global feminist community when the goal of women's sexual and reproductive rights, hard-won at the UN International Conference on Population and Development (IPCD) in Cairo, 1994, was excluded from the list. This omission is even more inexcusable given that the attainment of sexual and reproductive rights of women is not only a goal in itself, but a crucial target and/or indicator of progress under at least four of the other MDGs: Goal 3 (women's equality and empowerment), Goal 4 (child mortality), Goal 5 (maternal health), and Goal 6 (HIV/AIDS). The deliberate exclusion of this fundamental indicator of women's human rights and empowerment from the MDGs symbolises the new[2] power of religious fundamentalists, the lack of sincerity on the part of the majority of those who voted on them, and the struggle that lies ahead for anyone who seriously seeks equality, equity, and empowerment for women.

The exclusion of the goal of women's sexual and reproductive rights is an example of a major problem of the MDGs; namely, their abstraction from the social, political, and economic context in which they are to be implemented. The MDGs must be understood in the context of the emergence of the forces of economic and religious fundamentalisms that have followed the ending of the Cold War and the rise of political and religious conservatism. The political economy of the MDGs reflects the power of the forces of religious fundamentalism that emerged in the processes surrounding the 1994 Cairo Conference. These forces have continued to gain strength in the context of the ongoing economic struggles of the global South against the spread of neo-liberalism in the late 1990s, and they have received a boost through the right-wing control of the current US Administration.

In addition to the political context of the spread of religious fundamentalism and the male backlash against women's rights, there is the spread of economic fundamentalism, in the form of the neo-liberal agenda through the trade liberalisation enforced by the World Trade Organisation (WTO). For me, the major limitation of the MDGs lies in the fact that, in the official literature on these Goals, I can find almost no acknowledgement of the extent to which the neo-liberal policy framework, starting with the 1980s macro-economic policy framework of the Washington Consensus (including structural adjustment policies), is serving to halt and reverse progress towards the achievement of the Goals. In contrast, in the UN Development Decades of the 1960s and 1970s, and before the election of conservative governments in the USA and the UK, there was a widespread consensus around the aims enshrined today in the MDGs.

A limitation of the MDG approach which reflects economic fundamentalism is the formulation of Goal 8, which aims for the development of 'a global partnership for development' between governments and commercial corporations. This is considered highly problematic by many, who would argue that this is informed by a neo-liberal vision of development, which, far from being 'enabling', is profoundly 'disenabling', and jeopardises the achievement of the other Goals. This conclusion is shared even by individuals who initially gave support to the economic policies associated with the Washington Consensus,[3] and in particular the new trade agreements of the WTO.

To the extent that all the MDGs relate to the role of the state, one must ask how feasible it is that states weakened by the requirements of policy frameworks of neo-liberalism, and whose revenues are reduced by privatisation and trade liberalism, can be expected to achieve the goals and targets of the MDGs. The neo-liberal policy framework, with its emphasis on the market-friendly state (in contrast to the people-friendly state), has been reinforced by trade liberalisation and the new trade agreements enforced by the WTO. In the Caribbean, a consequence of trade liberalisation that has immediate relevance for the implementation of the MDGs in the region is the loss of government revenues resulting from the reduction in tariffs and the sale of profitable government assets. In Grenada, it has been calculated that more than 50 per cent of government revenue is derived from import duties.[4] How are governments to finance primary health care and basic education, when they are under pressure to reduce a major source of public finance?

Both religious and economic fundamentalisms rely on the subordination and exploitation of women's time, labour, and sexuality, for the benefit of patriarchal power on the one hand, and for the benefit of capitalism on the other. Thus, I cannot imagine a less 'enabling environment' for the promotion of policies and programmes for the achievement of women's equality and empowerment.

Women and the MDGs

Despite the limitations of the MDGs, however, women's advocates inside and outside the bureaucracies of governments and donors ought to use the opportunities the MDGs provide for advancing our agenda.

Since all the MDGs (with the exception of the last one) relate to biological and social reproduction, women's equality and empowerment are critical to their achievement. This fact provides women with an important opportunity for engagement in the policy dialogue around goals that have come to occupy a privileged position in the processes of socio-economic planning, and in the policy dialogue between governments and donors. The inclusion of goals and targets of major interest to women in the MDGs provides a chance to discuss and assess the barriers to the achievement of goals. To the extent that women's subordination and exploitation represent major barriers to the achievement of most of the goals and targets, the MDGs represent a tool with which to hold both donor agencies and governments accountable.

Goal 3, on gender equality and women's empowerment, is the goal to which women are expected to pay greatest attention. Space does not permit me to go into details about the problems associated with this goal. In particular, for the Caribbean, there are problems with its totally inadequate fourth target to 'eliminate gender disparity in primary and secondary education', using indicators as follows:

- the ratio of girls to boys in primary, secondary, and tertiary education (Indicator 9);

- the ratio of literate women to men in the 15–24 age group (Indicator 10);

- the share of women in wage employment in the non-agricultural sector (Indicator 11);

- the proportion of seats held by women in national parliaments (Indicator 12).

While the indicators on education and literacy represent major achievements for women everywhere, the Caribbean experience shows how inadequate they are as indicators of empowerment. Here in the Caribbean, the data show that girls outnumber boys at every level of education in almost all the countries of the English-speaking Caribbean (UNDP 2003). Yet this has not translated into higher access to employment, incomes, decision-making positions in the public domain, or political office. Moreover, despite efforts to change this, there is still a great deal of sex-role stereotyping in the school curriculum that limits the options of girls.

In the Caribbean, the worldwide backlash against advances in women's rights, and in particular the opposition to women's sexual and reproductive rights, has been paralleled and strengthened by the debates around the notion of 'male marginalisation'. As early as the 1980s, Errol Miller, a Professor of Education at UWI, drew attention to the overwhelming role of women in the education of boys in Jamaica (both in female-headed households in the homes, and in the schools where female teachers predominated) (Miller 1987). This sparked a public debate about the 'crisis' of Caribbean men and masculinity. Miller's second book, *Men at Risk*, reinforced this impression.[5] Currently, this debate is focusing on the perceived link between the 'underachievement' of Caribbean males in the education system and advances in the status of women as a major contributory factor. All of this undermines and derails women's activism.

Regarding the indicator on the number of women in parliaments, I would say that whether this is an indicator of women's empowerment depends on the circumstances under which women candidates take part in parliamentary elections. In Caribbean Community and Common Market (CARICOM) countries, with a few exceptions,[6] the small numbers of women who run for and win seats owe their preferment to the male decision makers within the political parties. Women who challenge male privilege are not likely to be among these. More importantly, once in office, women (and men) tend to cede their own power to that of their government, and are unlikely to have the freedom to make decisions about their lives and act upon them: in short, to demonstrate empowerment and agency, especially in relation to gender issues.

The inadequacy of these indicators for advancing the rights of Caribbean women can be judged from the fact that, apart from the indicator on women in parliaments, women in CARICOM countries have already achieved the targets. We've 'been there, and done that'. And yet, we can hardly speak of equality, equity, and empowerment in a situation where poverty persists, violence against women continues unabated,[7] there is increasing hostility against women (possibly generated by the very achievements in education and employment mentioned earlier), the spread of HIV / AIDS is the second most rapid after sub-Saharan Africa (and is spreading most quickly among women),[8] and where only two CARICOM countries (Barbados and Guyana) provide for abortion services that are accessible, safe, and affordable.

In UNIFEM's publication, *Progress of the World's Women 2000*, additional indicators of women's economic equality were proposed. These included tracking women's participation in informal wage work; capturing women's work in its entirety; and measuring the extent to which women are paid a living wage. In addition, UNIFEM has suggested that a target should be created to end gender disparity in wages. But while these measures are useful, they are still not adequate for the Caribbean region, which has one of the highest levels of literacy, education, and labour force participation in the world. The indicators of women's equality and empowerment in the Caribbean would have to include indicators on the incidence of rape

and domestic violence; access to health services that respect women's sexual and reproductive rights; access to and control of land; access to credit; and equality before the law.

Other important goals for CARICOM women

In my view, CARICOM women should pay as much attention to the gender dimensions of the other MDGs as they do to Goal 3. We have much more to gain from this approach. For the Caribbean region, Goals 1 (eradication of extreme poverty) and 6 (combating HIV / AIDS) should be prioritised, within a framework in which gender is seen as a cross-cutting issue. To the extent that both areas represent priorities for most CARICOM governments – in the way that gender equality and women's empowerment certainly do not – a focus on these Goals can be especially useful for CARICOM women.

However, there are problems with the formulation of the MDGs relating to poverty and HIV / AIDS; these need to be addressed if the framework of the MDGs is to be useful to women. One obvious problem is that the targets and indicators associated with these Goals are not disaggregated by gender.[9] Recognition of the disparity between men and women in terms of poverty, or the incidence of HIV / AIDS, is an important starting point for the design of effective policies, programmes, and strategies for addressing these areas.

Goal 1: poverty
Along with violence against women (not included as a target or indicator in the MDGs), poverty is one of the leading concerns identified by Caribbean women. The gender-blindness of the goal on income-poverty eradication is particularly problematic, especially as poverty is widely recognised as a 'highly gendered phenomenon, and in ways that are not captured by income or headcount

measures' (Subrahmanian 2003, 10). For Caribbean women, it is important to recognise that 'outcomes of poverty are embedded in processes and relations of gender' (ibid.), and that poverty reduction programmes must take these into account. For example, poverty reduction programmes must provide for a range of services, including low-income housing, access to water and sanitation, health services that integrate primary health care, maternal and child health, family planning, cancer detection, services for the detection and treatment of sexually transmitted diseases and HIV/AIDS, free and compulsory primary education, child-care provision, and women's access to credit, land, and skills training. They must also ensure that the minimum wage legislation extends to domestic workers and other categories of low-income work.

Because of the primary responsibility that women have for the care of children, elderly, sick, and disabled people, their income-earning capacity is more limited than that of men. It means that the incidence of poverty among women is greater than it is among men. This has particularly serious consequences in the Caribbean, where a high proportion of families are heavily or entirely dependent on the income of women, and there is a high incidence of female-headed households. In such a context, the earnings of women affect the well-being of entire families, and especially that of children and elderly people.

While poverty is a major concern for women, advocates should be aware of the tendency of governments and donors alike to 'collapse gender concerns within the wider category of poverty, as it enables the use of a fairly depoliticised and needs-based discourse as requiring focus on women within poor households, rather than gender disadvantage *per se*' (ibid. 11). This masks the uneven distribution of power and resources within households, especially when there are men present. Caribbean women know that when a man is present he receives the major share of food in the household, and his needs take priority over those of other household members. The assumption (often accepted by women themselves) that men are the 'heads of household' can work against the interests of women, who indeed carry the main responsibility for the care and maintenance of households.

A point of interest in the Caribbean is that women with limited resources often fare better in female-headed households than in one headed by a man. A study, by Lynn Bolles, of women in Jamaica during the economic crisis of the 1980s shows that when the woman is the sole bread-winner, a male partner is less likely than a second woman in the household to provide the assistance with domestic chores and child care that the working woman needs. If there is a second woman present, she not only assists with household maintenance tasks, but engages in her own income-generating activities, such as petty trading, crafts, or paid domestic work, to augment household income (Bolles 1983).

Finally, the link between gender equality, women's empowerment, and food security is critical in poor households: while Caribbean men can (and do) walk away from household responsibilities when they are not in a position to offer financial support, women stay and will do whatever it takes to put food on the table.

Goal 6: HIV/AIDS

The lack of attention to gender issues in Goal 6 and its associated indicators on the spread of HIV/AIDS is especially problematic. HIV/AIDS, like poverty, is a highly gendered phenomenon. Advocates ought to draw attention to the fact that women's sexual and reproductive rights must be the cornerstones to any effective programme for combating the spread of HIV/AIDS, even if this is presently excluded from the MDGs, with their targets and indicators. Central to the spread of HIV is the issue of sexuality and women's sexual and reproductive rights: no amount of education can protect a woman from exposure to the virus if she cannot negotiate safe sex.

As Sheila Stuart points out, young women and girls are particularly vulnerable when they engage in sex with older men, especially those in positions of authority, like clergymen, teachers, and employers (Stuart 2000). In the Caribbean, there is also a high incidence of incest, and the exposure of young girls to sexual assault by the male partners of their mothers is commonplace (ibid.). Finally, homophobia, especially in Jamaica (*New York Times* 2004), is an important factor in the spread of the virus. These are matters that should be discussed as part of any programme for combating the spread of HIV/AIDS in this region, and it is up to women to raise these questions. Unfortunately, the hostility and resentment shown by men towards women that underlies the 'male marginalisation' thesis in this region make open discussion of these issues especially difficult. This is hardly conducive to the kind of mutual respect and consideration necessary for the exercise of sexually responsible behaviour.

Two of the indicators of Goal 6 – the HIV/AIDS prevalence rates among pregnant women aged 15-24, and rates of condom use – are especially appropriate for this region. According to a Joint UN Programme on HIV/AIDS (UNAIDS) Fact Sheet of February 2001, in Trinidad and Tobago a large survey of men and women in their teens and early twenties showed that fewer than 20 per cent of sexually active respondents said they always used condoms, and two-thirds did not use condoms at all. Although the ratio of men to women living with HIV is 2:1 in the region, the rapid increase in HIV/AIDS among women can be gauged by the fact that this has increased from 5:1 in Barbados since the beginning of the disease in this country, and is now reported to be 1:1 (UNAIDS 2001). The ratio of 2:1 also conceals the ratio by age group. There is evidence that the rate of increase among young women may be higher than that of men in the same age group. According to the UNAIDS Fact Sheet, in Trinidad and Tobago HIV rates are reported to be five times higher in girls than in boys aged 15–18 years, and this is probably true of other countries in the region. Women's rights advocates should press for sex-disaggregated data in this area, and for a particular focus on these indicators.

Other goals and targets of special concern to women

Other goals and targets of special concern to women in the Caribbean are the reduction of the under-five mortality rate (Goal 4); improved maternal health (Goal 5); access to safe drinking water (Goal 7, Target 10); and improvements in the lives of slum dwellers (Goal 7, Target 11). Here, I confine myself to a few brief remarks regarding these goals in relation to the Caribbean. Overall, information, including statistics, is needed to indicate the extent, and reasons behind, the problems that these goals seek to address, as they exist in the Caribbean.

An example is the lack of information regarding Goals 4 and 5. While there were substantial improvements in infant and maternal mortality rates in the Caribbean in the 1960s and 1970s in the processes leading up to and following independence, there have been setbacks over the past two decades. These setbacks are the result of the onset of the HIV/AIDS pandemic, along with the deterioration in public health services. CARICOM governments had a good record throughout the 1960s and 1970s of making steady improvements in the provision of public health services. This has been placed in jeopardy with the pressures on states that came with the spread of neo-liberalism. It is important to assess the status of public health services in CARICOM countries at the present time, especially in the context of pressures to liberalise trade in services (through the proposed General Agreement on Trade in Services, or GATS).

There is a similar risk to public water supplies. It is difficult to reconcile the pressures of powerful government on poor countries to privatise water and liberalise trade in services with appearing to support the goals and targets of poverty reduction, access to safe drinking water, and improvements in the lives of slum dwellers.[10]

Regarding Goal 5, there are major problems with the indicators. To limit the indicator for the target of reducing maternal mortality rates by three-quarters to the 'proportion of births attended by skilled health personnel' is to ignore the importance of women's access to maternal and child health services, including family planning services. In the context of deteriorating public health services and the hostility of the current US Administration to the inclusion of abortion within family planning programmes and even to the use of condoms, this indicator is particularly inadequate.

Strategies to improve the MDGs

This section suggests some strategies to ensure that gender inequalities are identified and addressed in the MDG monitoring process, and in national policy responses from governments.

Holding governments to account through national and international monitoring of progress on gender issues

UNIFEM's special issue of *Progress of the World's Women 2002: Volume 2. Gender Equality and the Millennium Development Goals* (Elson with Keklik 2002) has a chapter on 'Innovations in measuring and monitoring', which focuses on improving national statistics, creating alternative indicators and indices, and producing supporting studies. Each region must identify indicators and devise strategies that accord with the resources and capabilities at its disposal.

However, as valuable as all these would be, they are meaningless without a strong and active women's movement to monitor those officials who are mandated to monitor. I am reminded of a project on gender-sensitive statistics undertaken by the Women's Desk of the CARICOM Secretariat some years ago. Despite the fact that the workshops were well attended by statistical officers from across the region, it would be hard to detect any marked improvement in the data available today.

There is really no *serious* commitment to collecting gender-disaggregated data, because there is little agreement on the importance of this issue. So far as the bureaucracies of the region are concerned, it seems to be sufficient for the governments to sign commitments, pledges, and conventions; taking action is another matter entirely. Even when there is action, it is so ineffective as to give credence to those who dismiss the whole issue of gender equality as a gimmick. I could give an entire paper on this, starting with my experience working with a government (Jamaica in the second half of the 1970s) that was at least semi-serious about women's equality and participation.[11] This was undoubtedly due to the fact that the women in the People's National Party (PNP) at that time, under the leadership of the wife of the Prime Minister and with the involvement of a number of wives of other ministers and officials, committed to the pursuit of an agenda for the advancement of women.

The UNIFEM report (Elson with Keklik 2002) also acknowledges that the achievement of the MDGs will require wide-based social mobilisation, including civil society, governments, and development agencies. It will also require women's organisations to actively monitor international and national progress towards Goal 3, and progress on all other Goals, with particular attention to gender issues.

Linking Gender Budgets to the MDGs

Another strategy worth examining is one that would link work on MDGs to work on Gender Budgets. The most effective work on Gender Budgets takes place at the level of civil society as well as within the bureaucracy. This work is just beginning in the Caribbean and, judging from experience in Latin America and elsewhere, there is much to be done to work out a mechanism that would ensure ongoing support for this within the bureaucracy. Here again, a link between those working on the inside and those on the outside is essential.

My own work in community development in the 1960s and 1980s, and currently with the Gender and Trade Network, suggests that economic literacy programmes which enable women and men at community level, and in NGOs, to understand how policy frameworks are influenced by global trends and agreements are an important base for the construction of proposals for policy alternatives which would lead to the achievement of goals such as poverty eradication, advances in education, improved health, and environmental protection – the MDGs.

A three-pronged approach to policy implementation at the national level

The discussion so far in this section reveals my view that since all the MDGs are political issues, and none more so than the goal of gender equality and women's empowerment, they will never be achieved if we continue to treat them as issues that can be addressed by purely technical means. No matter how good the indicators, no matter how accurate the statistics, nothing can be achieved without political will. A women's movement with an analysis of power and a set of carefully thought-through strategies is essential to the achievement of the MDGs.

My experience in setting up the Jamaican Women's Bureau in 1975 was that a three-pronged approach was essential for effective action. First, a well-placed and well-staffed mechanism is needed within the bureaucracy, with access to all government ministries. Bureaux of Gender Affairs or Women's Affairs have a crucial role to play in the monitoring and measurement of the implementation of the MDGs. Second, the links of these bureaux with key ministries – health, education, labour, finance and planning and foreign affairs – need to be strengthened. Political support is needed from feminists within the ministries and within the political parties, especially the governing party. Finally, in order to be effective, they have to build strong relationships with women's organisations, especially those with an activist orientation.

From my own experience in Jamaica, I found that, working together, these three groups of feminists in different institutional contexts were able to generate and initiate a fairly effective set of strategies that saw real advances in bureaucratic arrangements, legislation, and programmes within a relatively short period of time. In Jamaica, the first step was the appointment of an Adviser to the government on Women's Affairs early in 1974. Within one year, the women within the PNP were able to arrange for this single post to be converted into a Women's Desk in the Ministry of Social Welfare, and later into a Women's Bureau in the Office of the Prime Minister.

Linking the Beijing Platform for Action with the MDGs

To benefit from the high-profile attention received by the MDGs as the new consensus framework for development discourse and assistance, all those committed to the advancement of women's equality and empowerment need to develop strategies for monitoring and measuring progress towards the achievement of the Beijing Platform for Action, and building this into work on the MDGs. We must substitute the Best Plan of Action (BPA) for the Most Distracting Gimmick (MDG)! Certainly, in the Caribbean our resources are far too limited to have them spread over a number of 'initiatives' that are essentially no different from each other. The BPA includes all the concerns of the MDGs, and already has a constituency of support in an array of women's organisations, research and training centres, media and communications programmes, and international campaigns, not to mention mechanisms within bureaucracies at every level already working on the follow-up to the BPA.

Work has to be done to make the links between the MDGs and the BPA in terms of targets and indicators. New targets and indicators – drawn from the BPA – such as violence, gender equality in the labour force, time use, and so on may have to be added. Work is proceeding on the construction of new indices – in Africa, the United Nations Economic Commission for Africa (UNECA) is working on a Gender Status Index and an African Women's Progress Scoreboard, while in our own region, UNECLAC (the United Nations Economic Commission for Latin America and the Caribbean) is working on Indices of Fulfilled Commitments.

In sum, we need to develop an approach to the MDGs that would allow us to use a redefined goal of women's equality and empowerment as an entry point for addressing all the other MDGs. In this way, women's equality and empowerment might be seen for what it is: both an end and the means for making progress on all the MDGs. Moreover, all of this must be done in the awareness of the ways in which the spread of neo-liberalism, religious fundamentalism, and, in the Caribbean, male backlash places all the MDGs in jeopardy.

Peggy Antrobus has worked with governments and NGOs in the field of development since graduating with a degree in economics in 1958. She was a founding member of the network of Third World women, DAWN – Development Alternatives with Women for a New Era, (1984–6) and was its General Co-ordinator from 1991 –6. Her book, The Global Women's Movement: Origins, Strategies and Challenges, *was recently published by Zed Books. Address: 4 Valley View, Frere Pilgrim, Christ Church, Barbados. E-mail: pan@caribsurf.com.*

Notes

1 This paper is drawn from a presentation to the Working Group on the MDGs and Gender Equality, at the UNDP Caribbean Regional Millennium Development Goals (MDGs) Conference, in Barbados, 7–9 July 2003.

2 It is 'new' since the ascendancy of a US Administration that is heavily influenced by the religious right. In 1994, the US Administration stood squarely with the women's movement in advancing women's reproductive rights.

3 The Washington Consensus is a set of policies adopted by indebted nations, intended to assist governments in paying off foreign debt. The policies aim to cut government expenditures, promote the private sector, and boost exports. The package includes cuts in government subsidies and social services, privatisation of assets and services, deregulation and liberalisation of the economy, and currency devaluation.

4 This statement was made by an official from the Ministry of Trade at a regional meeting on trade held in Grenada in 1999. Actual data should be available from the Caribbean Development Bank.

5 I am grateful to Tracy Robinson of the Faculty of Law, Cave Hill Campus, UWI, for pointing out to me that quite a bit of what we attribute to Miller is either not included in those two monographs, but in public conversations in the press and speeches, or it represents what his work has been taken to mean: 'there are at least two kinds of feminist analyses of Miller's work: one critiquing Miller directly, and the other speaking more broadly about the impact of his thesis' (personal communication). Nevertheless, the combination of the publications with their evocative/provocative titles has spawned a 'thesis' that has encouraged a critique of the supposed privileging of women in the region, which has undermined advocacy for women's rights in the region (see Barriteau 2000, 2003a, 2003b).

6 The exceptions are those women who are too powerful to be ignored – women like Eugenia Charles in Dominica, Portia Simpson in Jamaica, and Billie Miller and Mia Mottley in Barbados. However, none of these identified themselves with the political agendas for women's equality.

7   It is notoriously difficult to get accurate data on this. Roberta Clarke's (1998) report, *Violence Against Women in the Caribbean*, prepared for UNIFEM and the Inter-American Commission of Women, highlights the problem.

8   Within three years of the report of the first case of AIDS, female and paediatric cases represented 23 per cent of the total. There is now parity between the number of men and women with AIDS, and the spread of HIV/AIDS among young women aged 15–24 is the highest for any age group (see Stuart 2000).

9   Of course, disaggregation is not without its problems, as Diane Elson warns us: 'the basic problem with disaggregation is that it focuses on the separate characteristics of men or women, rather than the social institutions of gender as a power relation' (Elson 1998, 160).

10 There is a Caribbean Gender and Trade Network (CGTN), part of the International Gender and Trade Network, which monitors the trade negotiations and is an important source of information. The programme of the CGTN also includes research and economic/trade literacy (see www.igtn.org). These are resources available to women's organisations in this region.

11 A full account of this experience is in my Lucille Mair Lecture, delivered at the Mona Campus, UWI, in 2000, which is the basis of my chapter in the book, *Developing Power: How Women Transformed International Development* (Fraser and Tinker 2004).

References

Barriteau, E. (2000) *Examining the Issues of Men, Male Marginalisation and Masculinity in the Caribbean: Policy Implications*, Cave Hill Working Paper Series No. 4, Centre for Gender and Development Studies, UWI

Barriteau, E. (2003a) 'Requiem for the male marginalization thesis in the Caribbean: death of a non-theory', in E. Barriteau (ed.) *Confronting Power, Theorising Gender: Interdisciplinary Perspectives in the Caribbean*, Kingston: UWI Press

Barriteau, E. (2003b) 'Conclusion: beyond a blacklash: the frontal assault on containing Caribbean women in the decade of the 1990s', in G. Tang Nain and B. Bailey (eds.) *Gender Equality in the Caribbean: Reality or Illusion*, Kingston: Ian Randle Publishers

Bolles, L. (1983) 'Kitchens hit by priorities: employed working-class Jamaican women confront the IMF', in J. Nash and M.P. Fernandez-Kelly (eds.) *Women, Men, and the International Division of Labor*, New York: State University of New York Press

Clarke, R. (1998) *Violence Against Women in the Caribbean: State and Non-state Response*, UNIFEM and the Inter-American Commission of Women (CIM)

Elson, D. with H. Keklik (2002) *Progress of the World's Women 2002: Volume 2. Gender Equality and the Millennium Development Goals*, New York: UNIFEM

Fraser, A. and I. Tinker (eds.) (2004) *Developing Power: How Women Transformed International Development*, The Feminist Press

ICRW (2003) 'Promises to Keep', Task Force Background Paper on Gender Equality and Women's Empowerment, www.unmillenniumproject.org

Miller, E. (1987) *The Marginalisation of the Caribbean Male: Insights from the Development of the Teaching Profession*

New York Times (2004) ' "Hated to death" in Jamaica', editorial, 2 December 2004

Stuart, S. (2000) 'The reproductive health challenge: women and AIDS in the Caribbean', in G. Howe and A. Cobley (eds.) *The Caribbean AIDS Epidemic*, Kingston: UWI Press

Subrahmanian, R. (2003) 'Promoting gender equality', in R. Black and H. White (eds.) *Targeting Development*, London: Routledge

UNAIDS (2001) *HIV/AIDS Fact Sheet*, February

UNDP (2003) 'Caribbean Regional Report on the Implementation of the Millennium Development Goals', unpublished paper prepared for the UNDP Caribbean Office

Resources

Compiled by Kanika Lang

Publications

Gender Mainstreaming in Poverty Eradication and the Millennium Development Goals: A Handbook for Policy-makers and Other Stakeholders (2003), Naila Kabeer, Commonwealth Secretariat, Marlborough House, Pall Mall, London SW1Y 5HX, UK. http://publications.thecommonwealth.org Also available online at: www.thecommonwealth.org/shared_ asp_files/uploadedfiles/{EEEA4F53-90DF-4498-9C58-73F273F1E5EE}_ PovertyEradication.pdf

In this book, Kabeer provides evidence for the crucial importance of gender equality to the attainment of all the MDGs. The book highlights the importance of understanding the gendered dimensions of poverty and emphasises that two key factors in poverty reduction are increasing women's access to resources and recognising the importance of women's economic contributions to the survival of poor households around the world. She also demonstrates the interrelationship between gender equality, economic growth, and the attainment of the human development indicators targeted in the MDGs. Central to her discussion is the importance of cultural norms, kinship patterns, and structures of patriarchy in the regional manifestation of gender inequalities and the impact of economic growth on gender equality. Kabeer also examines the specific MDG on gender equality against women's access to education, literacy, paid work, and political representation and concludes that these resources are important but not sufficient for women's empowerment.

Progress of the World's Women 2002: Volume 2. Gender Equality and the Millennium Development Goals (2002), Diane Elson with Hande Keklik, UNIFEM. Can be ordered from Women, Ink, 777 United Nations Plaza, New York, NY 10017, USA. wink@womenink.org
Order online at: http://womenink.org/ or from Kumarian Press at: www.kpbooks.com. Also available free online at: www.unifem.org/index.php?f_page_pid=10

The report assesses the progress made by countries of the world in achieving Millennium Development Goal 3, on gender equality and the empowerment of women, against the four specific indicators of education (secondary-school enrolment), literacy, employment (non-agricultural wage employment), and seats in parliament. It also discusses the importance of creating and using innovative new sex-disaggregated indicators that better capture dimensions of women's disadvantage. The report also highlights the omission of women's inclusion in Goal 8 (achieving a global partnership for development) and argues the case for bottom–up partnerships that hold governments and corporations accountable rather than the current top–down partnerships envisioned by the Goal.

Seeking Accountability on Women's Human Rights: Women Debate the Millennium Development Goals (2004), Carol Barton and Laurie Prendergast (eds.), Women's International Coalition for Economic Justice (WICEJ), 12 Dongan Place #206, New York, NY 10040, USA.
www.wicej.org
Hard copies are available from info@wicej.org (please include your full mailing address).

Featuring 29 articles and short opinion pieces from women in diverse roles (from civil society, human rights organisations, and academia) and regions of the world (including Russia, Tanzania, and Colombia), this book presents diverse viewpoints on women's engagement with the MDGs. It includes sections on the importance of a human rights perspective on the MDGs, understanding the MDGs within wider frameworks such as international law, strategies for engaging with the MDGs and transforming them as a tool for rights, equality, sustainable development, and peace. The book aims to serve as an accessible tool to enable women's organisations to assess how, why, and whether to engage with the MDGs.

Pathway to Gender Equality: CEDAW, Beijing and the MDGs (2004), Lee Waldorf, UNIFEM. Available online at: www.unifem.org/index.php?f_page_pid=216

This report looks at the linkages and crossovers among the MDGs, the Convention on the Elimination of All Forms of Discrimination Against Women (CEDAW) and the Beijing Platform for Action; and argues that the MDGs should not be viewed as a new agenda but as a new means of attaining CEDAW and Beijing. Conversely, ensuring that the commitments made in CEDAW and Beijing are fulfilled would help in the attainment of the MDGs. The report provides practical guidelines on how to link the MDGs processes with CEDAW and Beijing.

Gender, the Millennium Development Goals, and Human Rights in the Context of the 2005 Review Processes (2004), Genevieve Renard Painter, Gender and Development Network (GADN), c/o WOMANKIND Worldwide, 2nd Floor, Development House, 56–64 Leonard Street, London EC2A 4JX, UK.
Available online at www.siyanda.org/docs/painter_cedawmdgs.doc

This paper was written by Painter to inform the Gender and Development Network's advocacy strategy for 2005. Painter highlights the opportunities for advocacy presented by linking and participating in the MDG Review process and the Beijing Platform for Action +10 Review process. She argues that it is vital to conceptualise the MDGs from a human rights perspective and explores the links between CEDAW, the Beijing Platform for Action, and the MDGs.

'Promoting gender equality' by Ramya Subrahmanian, in *Targeting Development: Critical Perspectives on the Millennium Development Goals*, Richard Black and Howard White (eds.), Routledge, Taylor & Francis Group, 2 Park Square, Milton Park, Abingdon, Oxford, OX14 4RN, UK (2004).
www.routledge.com

Subrahmanian critically examines MDG 3 on gender equality and empowerment, and argues that the targets and indicators of the Goal may specify outcomes/ends, but they fail to make clear what routes/processes are necessary to achieve these outcomes. She also makes the point that the notion of gender empowerment that the MDGs adopt seems to be restricted only to health and education goals, and criticises the gender-blindness of the poverty eradication goal as a major shortcoming. In order to achieve gender equality, Subrahmanian emphasises that all the major actors in development must ensure transparency in all levels of their policy processes.

Taking Action: Achieving Gender Equality and Empowering Women (Final Report of the UN Millennium Project Task Force on Education and Gender Equality) (2005), Caren Grown, Geeta Rao Gupta, and Aslihan Kes, Earthscan, 8–12 Camden High Street, London NW1 0JH, UK
earthinfo@earthscan.co.uk
www.earthscan.co.uk
Available online at:
http://unmp.forumone.com/eng_task_force/GenderEbook.pdf

The Final Report by the Task Force on Education and Gender Equality spells out the seven strategic priorities that are essential in order to achieve gender equality and women's empowerment by 2015. These are strengthening opportunities for post-primary education for girls, guaranteeing reproductive and sexual health and rights, investing in infrastructure to reduce women's and girls' time-burden, guaranteeing women's and girls' property and inheritance rights, eliminating gender inequality in employment by decreasing women's reliance on informal employment, increasing women's share of seats in local and national government, and combating violence against women and girls. The report stresses, however, that gender equality cannot and will not be achieved without the leadership to institute policies for social change and the political will to allocate the necessary resources towards their fulfilment.

Common Ground: Women's Access to Natural Resources and the United Nations Millennium Development Goals (2003), Rebecca Pearl, Women's Environment and Development Organization (WEDO), 355 Lexington Avenue, 3rd Floor, New York, NY 10017-6003, USA.
wedo@wedo.org
www.wedo.org
The booklet can be ordered from WEDO using their online order form at:
www.wedo.org/publicat/shop.htm
and is also available free online at:
www.wedo.org/sus_dev/common1.htm

This booklet demonstrates the links between Goal 1 (poverty eradication), Goal 3 (gender equality and the empowerment of women), and Goal 7 (environmental sustainability) in the context of increasing women's access to natural resources. Four key dimensions frame the discussion, along with accompanying case studies: water (Kenya), energy (Malawi), land and food security (Tanzania and Nepal), and biodiversity (Kenya and Laos). Recommended strategies, tools, and actions to ensure the links between gender and access to natural resources are incorporated into the MDG process at a national level include the use of sex-disaggregated data, gender reviews of country reports, and gender budget initiatives.

80 Million Lives: Meeting the Millennium Development Goals in Child and Maternal Survival (2003), Suzanne Fustukian, Regina Keith, and Angela Penrose, Grow Up Free from Poverty Coalition.
Available free online at:
www.savethechildren.org.uk/temp/scuk/cache/cmsattach/1527_80millionlives.pdf
or by writing to: Save the Children, 17 Grove Lane, London, SE5 8RD, UK.

This report, by a UK-based coalition of NGOs, faith groups, young people's organizations, and civil society organisations, focuses on Goal 4 (reducing child mortality) and Goal 5 (improving maternal health), arguing that a 'social mode' of health-care provision is vital to the attainment of these Goals. The report is based on a rights-based approach to health care. It sets out the Coalition's recommendations on how to implement a 'health for all' system. The title of the report derives from the fact that achieving the MDGs by 2015 will help to save 80m children and women from death.

'Strategic advocacy and maternal mortality: moving targets and the Millennium Development Goals', Lynn Freedman, in *Women Reinventing Globalisation*, Caroline Sweetman and Joanna Kerr (eds.), Oxfam

GB, 274 Banbury Road, Oxford, OX2 7DZ, UK (2003).

Available online at:
http://publications.oxfam.org.uk/oxfam/default.asp

Freedman stresses the importance of access to Emergency Obstetric Care, in the event of birth complications, as vital to the achievement of the MDG on the reduction of maternal mortality. She argues that this MDG provides an important avenue for strategic advocacy to attain accountable health systems that can deliver the care necessary to save women's lives and improve their health.

Gender and Education For All: The Leap to Equality. EFA Global Monitoring Report 2003/4 (2003) UNESCO.

Can be ordered online at:
www.publishing.unesco.org

or downloaded at:
http://portal.unesco.org/education/en/ ev.php-URL_ID=23023&URL_DO= DO_TOPIC&URL_SECTION=201.html

The report assesses the progress made towards the six Education For All goals, adopted at the World Education Forum in Dakar, Senegal in 2000, two of which were later incorporated into the Millennium Development Goals of education and gender equity. Stressing the importance of achieving gender equality in education from a human rights perspective, the report makes a distinction between gender parity in education (a numerical concept) and gender equality (a more complex notion including equal learning achievements and the life opportunities that follow). The report is divided into seven chapters, which examine through a gender lens, towards achieving the goalsthe barriers to the attainment of gender equality, examples of good practice, and the national and international strategies and commitments that will be necessary in order to make gender equality in education a reality.

Gender, Education and Development: Beyond Access to Empowerment (1999), Christine Heward and Sheila Bunwaree (eds.), Zed Books, 7 Cynthia Street, London N1 9JF, UK www.zedbooks.co.uk

This book draws on case studies from Ethiopia, Sri Lanka, Malaysia, South Africa, Tanzania, Pakistan, Nepal, Mauritius, Niger, Peru, and Papua New Guinea to argue that education does not automatically lead to the empowerment of women. For example, the case study from Sri Lanka demonstrates that equal educational attainment does not translate into equal rewards in the labour market for women. Social, cultural, political, and economic factors all affect the impact of education on the lives of girls and women. The book also contains a strong critique of the World Bank's education policy as simplistic and unresponsive to the realities of the lives of poor and marginalised girls and women the world over.

Partnerships for Girls' Education (2005), Nitya Rao and Ines Smyth (eds.), Oxfam GB, 274 Banbury Road, Oxford, OX2 7DZ, UK.

By documenting and analysing the achievements and challenges of a multitude of partnerships for girls' education, this book aims to suggest strategies for progress towards the achievement of the Millennium Development Goals. An account of the formation and development of the Global Campaign for Education is followed by detailed case studies from Bangladesh, Egypt, the Philippines, Peru, and sub-Saharan Africa, illustrating a wide range of partnerships and raising crucial questions about power and control, 'scaling up', and sustainability.

The Beijing Platform for Action and the Millennium Development Goals: How to Defend the Progress Made? How to Move Forward in Globalising Women's Rights: Confronting Unequal Development Between the UN Rights Framework and the WTO Trade Agreements (2004) Women In Development Europe

(WIDE) Annual Conference Report, pp 51–7. Can be ordered by sending an e-mail to Nerea Craviotto at info@wide-network.org

This section of the WIDE Annual Conference Report contains presentations by Kalyani Menon-Sen and Carol Barton. The presentations provide concise critiques of the MDGs from the perspective of the women's movement (for example the relegation of gender to only one Goal, and the inadequate measures of the complex notion of 'empowerment') and explore the links between the MDGs and the Beijing Platform for Action. They also discuss some of the strategies being adopted by the women's movement for 2005.

Websites

Gender Equality and the MDGs
This site is managed by the United Nations Development Fund for Women (UNIFEM) and is a result of collaboration among the UN's Inter-Agency Network on Women and Gender Equality, the OECD/DAC Network on Gender Equality, and the Multilateral Development Bank Working Group on Gender. It aims to provide a pool of online resources and tools that address gender equality in all of the eight Millennium Development Goals. It features online books, papers, articles, and speeches as well as downloadable leaflets and pamphlets for advocacy and action, and links to other relevant organisations. Visitors to the site may submit materials for inclusion by e-mailing the content manager (contact details and guidelines for submission are provided).

Beyond Access
www.girlseducation.org (click on the Beyond Access Project link)

This is the website of the 'Gender, Development and Education: Beyond Access' Project, funded by the UK's Department for International Development, and co-ordinated by Elaine Unterhalter of the Institute of Education, London and Sheila Aikman of Oxfam GB. The Project was launched in April 2003 and will run until December 2005. It is linked to work in support of the Millennium Development Goal for gender equity in education worldwide by 2005. The main aims of the Project are to share new knowledge, critically examine practice, and undertake new strategies for learning between policy makers, NGOs, intergovernment organisations, practitioners, academics, teachers, and the general public and build awareness of debates and practical strategies for the delivery of gender equitable education through a series of seminars, a conference, and a range of publications.

The Millennium Development Goals (UN Millennium Project website)
www.unmillenniumproject.org/html/dev_goals1.shtm

Information on the eight Goals and the Goal-specific targets and indicators.

Millennium Project
www.unmillenniumproject.org/html/about.shtm

The Millennium Project, launched by UN Secretary-General Kofi Annan and UNDP Administrator Mark Malloch Brown, is a three-year effort to identify strategies for meeting the MDGS, including identifying priorities, strategies, organisational means, and financing structures. The purpose of the Project is to ensure that all developing countries meet the MDGs. Ten Task Forces, comprising representatives from academia, public and private sectors, and civil society organisations, have been organised to carry out analytical work on the Project, prepare reports on progress, and provide recommendations on how to achieve the Goals.

Millennium Indicators database
http://millenniumindicators.un.org/unsd/mi/mi_goals.asp

An online database with country-specific information on progress towards the MDGs.

Millennium Development Goals – Country Reports
www.undp.org/mdg/countryreports.html

Reports from 62 countries including Afghanistan, Honduras, Zambia, Vietnam, and Slovenia on progress towards the MDGs.

Electronic resources

Gender Equality, Poverty Eradication and the Millennium Development Goals: Promoting Women's Capabilities and Participation (2003), Naila Kabeer, Emerging Social Issues Division, United Nations Economic and Social Commission on Asia and the Pacific (UNESCAP)
www.unescap.org/esid/GAD/Publication/DiscussionPapers/13/Paper13.pdf

In this paper, Kabeer emphasises that gender inequality is a pervasive form of inequality that is firmly a part of the structural inequalities that give rise to the problems the MDGs are designed to address, and therefore addressing gender inequalities in all of the MDGs is crucial. She critiques the omission of gender-specific aspects of the Goals, and in particular, Goal 1's failure to make explicit mention of the gender dimensions of poverty. Kabeer then goes on to examine each of the indicators that have been set to measure progress towards Goal 3 (gender equality and the empowerment of women) – education, employment, and political participation – and, while acknowledging the importance of these targets, stresses the influential role that culture can play in the attainment of these indicators for women and girls around the world. She concludes by stressing the importance of women's collective action as a basis for challenging existing structural inequalities.

Women and the Millennium Development Goals (2003), Ana Elena Obando, WHRnet (Women's Human Rights Net)
www.whrnet.org/docs/issue-mdg.html

This online paper reviews some of the main responses by the international women's movement to the MDGs. It highlights the criticisms of the MDGs by the women's movement (for example failure to include sexual and reproductive rights, failure to recognise neo-liberal context, and diminished state control), the challenges posed to the women's movement by the MDGs process (for example, ensuring that gender-sensitive indicators are adopted at a national level), and the opportunities that the MDGs present to the international women's movement (opportunities for the analysis of the barriers faced by women that would prevent the successful attainment of the Goals).

Gender and the MDGs (2004), Caren Grown, Asian Development Bank
www.adb.org/Documents/Periodicals/ADB_Review/2004/vol36_1/gender_mdgs.asp

Grown, the Director of the Poverty Reduction and Economic Growth Team, International Center for Research on Women (ICRW), sets out four priorities necessary to accelerate progress towards Goal 3: first, achieving gender equality in education, health, labour markets, political life, and social opportunities; second, investing in the education, health, safety, and economic well-being of adolescents, especially girls; third, reducing women's and girls' time poverty through gender-sensitive infra-structure investments and public policies that support women's care responsibilities; and fourth, sex-disaggregated data to monitor progress towards the MDGs.

Promises to Keep: Achieving Gender Equality and the Empowerment of Women', Background Paper of the Task Force on Education and Gender Equality (2003), Caren Grown, Geeta Rao Gupta, and Zahia Khan, UN Millennium Project, UNDP www.unmillenniumproject.org/documents/tf03genapr18.pdf

This is the first Background Paper for the Task Force on Education and Gender Equality, a part of the UN Millennium Project. The paper reviews the progress that countries have made on Goal 3. It is divided into six sections: Section 1 defines gender equality and empowerment (in terms of capability, opportunity, and agency); Section 2 provides a history of the development of Goal 3 and discusses its importance in relation to the other MDGs; Section 3 critiques the targets and indicators selected for the Goal and suggests more adequate ones; Section 4 analyses progress made by countries to reach the Goal; and Sections 5 and 6 identify strategic ways to meet Goal 3 by suggesting policy and programme interventions appropriate for different countries, based on the dominant form of discrimination experienced by women. The report concludes by urging the international community to ensure that four key prerequisites to achieving Goal 3 are met: quality, sex disaggregated data, financial and technical resources, international mechanisms and political will.

Task Force 3 Interim Report on Gender Equality (2004), Nancy Birdsall, Amina J. Ibrahim, and Geeta Rao Gupta, Millennium Project, UNDP
www.unmillenniumproject.org/documents/tf3genderinterim.pdf

This Interim Report builds on the analysis of the Task Force's Background Paper *Promises to Keep* (referenced above) on the progress towards Goal 3. This report presents a definition of gender equality using three dimensions – capabilities, access to resources and opportunities, and security – and reviews the progress made towards Goal 3 based on the adopted targets and indicators. Concluding that these targets and indicators are inadequate, the report identifies six strategic priorities (opportunities for secondary education, sexual and repro-

ductive rights and health, reducing women's and girls' time poverty, women's property and inheritance and labour market rights, women's political representation, and ending violence against women) that must be addressed through international- and national-level actions, and with two key sub-populations in particular – poor women and adolescents and youth – if progress is to be made on achieving gender equality and the empowerment of women.

The Economic and Human Development Costs of Missing the Millennium Development Goals on Gender Equity (2004), Dina Abu-Ghaida and Stephan Klasen, Discussion Paper, Department of Economics, University of Munich
www1.worldbank.org/education/pdf/MDG_Gender_Equity.pdf
http://epub.ub.uni-muenchen.de/archive/00000002/01/0301_klasen.pdf

Drawing on current findings on the relationship between gender equality (in terms of girls' education) and economic growth, the authors discuss the cost implications for countries that will miss the MDG on gender equality. They conclude that countries that fail to achieve Goal 3 will suffer significant losses in terms of forgone economic growth and will make less progress in reducing levels of fertility, child mortality, and under-nutrition. Girls' education, say the authors, is therefore significant not only in order to close the gender gap within a country but also for the overall development of the country.

Millennium Development Goals. National Reports: A Look Through a Gender Lens (2003), Kalyani Menon-Sen, UNDP, 1 United Nations Plaza, New York, NY 10017, USA
www.undp.org/gender/docs/mdgs-genderlens.pdf

This UNDP paper reviews the Millennium Development Goals Reports of 13 countries to assess the extent to which gender equality perspectives have been mainstreamed within the Reports. It finds that gender has not been sufficiently and effectively incorporated within the analyses. Suggestions for improvement include the inclusion of disaggregated data and qualitative information on critical gender issues across goals and targets. The countries covered are Albania, Armenia, Bolivia, Cameroon, Egypt, Lithuania, Mauritius, Mozambique, Nepal, Poland, Saudi Arabia, Tanzania, and Viet Nam. This paper provides concrete evidence on how countries are failing to take gender issues into account in their reporting on the MDGs.

Indicators for Monitoring the Millennium Development Goals: Definitions, Rationale, Concepts, and Sources (2003), United Nations Development Group
www.mdgender.net/upload/tools/Indicators_for_Monitoring_the_MDGs.pdf
This handbook provides guidance on the definitions, rationale, concepts, and sources of data for each of the indicators that are used to monitor the MDG targets. For each indicator used to measure progress towards the targets and goals, the handbook provides a simple operational definition, the goal and target that it addresses, the rationale for use of the indicator, the method of computation, sources of data, references including relevant websites, periodicity of measurement, gender and disaggregation issues, limitations of the indicator, and national and international agencies involved in the collection, compilation or dissemination of the data.

Gender Equality and the Millennium Development Goals (2003), Gender and Development Group, World Bank, 1818 H Street NW, Washington DC 20433, USA
http://siteresources.worldbank.org/INTGENDER/Publications/20169280/gendermdg.pdf
Drawing on research that builds a global picture of the current status of women's legal, political, economic, and social rights, this paper by the Gender and Development Group of the World Bank examines the gender equality Millennium Development Goal as well as the links between gender equality and the achievement of the poverty, education, health and nutrition, and environment Goals. While it does not critically examine the World Bank's own policies, it does argue strongly for the need to attain gender equality in order to achieve the other MDGs, and discusses Goal-specific gender-sensitive approaches that would enable the implementation of the Goals.

Reproductive Health and Gender Equality: Paper for the Task Force on Education and Gender Equality (2003), Carmen Barroso and Françoise Girard
www.mdgender.net/upload/monographs/ReproductiveHealth_and_GenderEquality_1.doc
The authors highlight the failure of Goal 3 on gender equality to address women's right to reproductive health, arguing that reproductive health and access to health care are essential for gender equality. They urge the Millennium Project's Task Force on Education and Gender Equality to include targets and indicators on reproductive health as central to gender equality.

The Cost of Childbirth: How Women are Paying the Price for Broken Promises on Aid, Oxfam Briefing Paper (2004), Oxfam GB, 274 Banbury Road, Oxford, OX2 7DZ, UK
www.oxfam.org.uk/what_we_do/issues/debt_aid/downloads/bp52_childbirth.pdf
This paper argues that, on current trends, the Millennium Development Goal on reducing maternal mortality by two-thirds by 2015 will be missed. This failing, say the authors, can be rectified if donors increase their aid for financing of better health-care provisions and governments ensure that health systems are responsive to the needs of women.

Engendering the Millennium Development Goals on Health (2003), Department of Gender and Women's Health, World Health Organization (WHO)
www.mdgender.net/upload/monographs/WHO_MDGs_on_Health.pdf

This leaflet highlights gender-specific concerns related to the health MDGs (1, 4, 5, 6, and 7) and identifies factors that programme planners and researchers should bear in mind to ensure that the concerns are addressed.

Promoting the Millennium Development Goal for Gender Equality in Education: Reflections from the Beyond Access Project (2004), Chloe Challender and Elaine Unterhalter, Institute of Education, University of London
http://k1.ioe.ac.uk/schools/efps/GenderEducDev/Cuba%20paper.pdf

This paper discusses the Beyond Access Project, set up in 2003 to facilitate dialogue and knowledge-sharing around the education MDG. It sets out the Project's 'scorecard methodology' to assess the progress made by countries towards the Goal, and the Project's aim of joining up top-level (international and government) work and consensus on the Goal with the grassroots-level work.

Gender and Education For All: The Leap to Equality. Commissioned Papers (2003)
http://portal.unesco.org/education/en/ev.php-URL_ID=25755&URL_DO=DO_TOPIC&URL_SECTION=201.html

More than 70 Background Papers on gender and education informed the EFA Global Monitoring Report 2003/4 (see the Publications section for further details). Major barriers to education are analysed in papers on child labour, school fees, and HIV/AIDS. Others shed light on the household perspective, teaching profession, disability, and the issue of gender violence in school. Some papers locate education within the broader context of globalisation and political participation. Country-specific information on progress towards gender equality in education is presented in papers from all around the world including Nigeria, Chile, Jamaica, France, the UK, Chad, Benin, and India.

The Beyond Access Project Seminar Papers
www.girlseducation.org/PGE_Active_Pages/NetworkMembers/BeyondAccess/Active_Pages/eventsandactivities.asp

The website provides access to all the papers discussed at the Beyond Access Project seminars. Themes include developing gender equality in adult education, resources for gender equality and quality basic education, and gender equality and basic education: ideas and actions. To read the papers for each seminar, go to 'click here for papers'.

Equals: The Beyond Access Project Newsletter
www.girlseducation.org/PGE_Active_Pages/NetworkMembers/BeyondAccess/Active_Pages/newsletter.asp

Link to the bi-monthly newsletter produced by the Project in order to share information and analysis and discuss latest developments in international efforts towards attaining gender equality in education.

Learning to Survive: How Education For All Would Save Millions of Young People from HIV/AIDS (2004) Oxfam
www.oxfam.org.uk/what_we_do/issues/education/downloads/gce_hivaids.pdf

An Oxfam report which stresses that education for all would prove to be a crucial 'vaccine' against HIV/AIDS. The report looks in particular at the benefits of education for young women in protecting them against the virus. Education, argues the report, provides young women with access to knowledge, economic resources, and decision-making power that deeply affects their ability to protect themselves against HIV/AIDS.

A Fair Chance: Attaining Gender Equality in Basic Education by 2005 (2003) Oxfam
www.oxfam.org.uk/what_we_do/issues/education/downloads/gce_afairchance_full.pdf

This accessible report by Oxfam draws on nine case studies to examine the current gender gap in education and the barriers to girls' education, including early marriage, user fees, son preference, heavy workloads at home, lack of adequate government schools, and sexual abuse in schools. It then goes on to suggest strategies that would enable countries to close the gender gap, such as free basic education, subsidies for girls' education for the poorest families, protection of the rights and dignity of girls in school, and increased aid for education. The report argues for the urgent need to tackle gender-specific discrimination and a country-level strategy for gender equality in education.

Gender and Budgets: Cutting Edge Pack (2003) BRIDGE
www.bridge.ids.ac.uk/reports_gend_CEP.html#Budgets

This pack provides information on how budgets can be used as a tool to further gender equality. It includes an overview report on gender budget initiatives and the processes involved, a collection of supporting resources that provide summaries of key texts, case studies, tools, and organisations and a bulletin that discusses how gender budget initiatives are a practical tool to advance towards gender equity.

The Convention on the Elimination of All Forms of Discrimination Against Women (CEDAW) and its Monitoring Mechanisms: Challenges and Opportunities for NGOs in their Efforts to Globalize Women's Human Rights (2004), Dr Hanna Beate Schoepp-Schilling at the Women In Development Europe (WIDE) Annual Conference 2004
www.eurosur.org/wide/Structure/CBS4_

UN_1.htm#top

As many women's organisations argue, in the light of the inadequacy of the MDGs from a women's human rights perspective, the Convention on the Elimination of All Forms of Discrimination Against Women represents vital legal protection of women's human rights. This speech, delivered by Dr Schoepp-Schilling at WIDE's 2004 Annual Conference, explains what CEDAW is and provides examples of the kind of monitoring work that NGOs can undertake to ensure that CEDAW represents a strong instrument for the protection of women's rights.

The Convention on the Elimination of All Forms of Discrimination Against Women
www.un.org/womenwatch/daw/cedaw/cedaw.htm

The UN website with the history and full text of the CEDAW. States that have ratified the Convention are legally bound to undertake a series of measures to end discrimination against women in all forms, including incorporating the principle of equality of men and women in their legal system; abolishing all discriminatory laws and adopting appropriate ones prohibiting discrimination against women; establishing tribunals and other public institutions to ensure the effective protection of women against discrimination; and ensuring elimination of all acts of discrimination against women by persons, organisations, or enterprises.

Beijing Platform for Action (2004), Carol Barton

www.eurosur.org/wide/Structure/CBS4_UN_2.htm

The Beijing Platform for Action was adopted at the Fourth UN World Conference on Women in Beijing, China in 1995. Carol Barton provides a concise summary of the Beijing Platform for Action and its strengths, weaknesses, and contradictions. Barton sheds light on the background of backlash against which women's rights activists are now being forced to defend the Platform, despite its many limitations.

Beijing Declaration and Platform for Action (1995)

www.un.org/womenwatch/daw/beijing/platform/

The UN website that provides the full text of the Beijing Declaration and the Platform for Action, including the 12 strategic objectives and actions that women's organisations argue are more representative of women's rights than the MDGs.

Tools for advocacy

Women's Empowerment, Gender Equality and the Millennium Development Goals: A WEDO Information and Action Guide (2004), Women's Environment and Development Organization (WEDO)

www.wedo.org/publicat/MDG_toolkit1.pdf

This leaflet provides Goal-specific reasons for the centrality of gender issues to the attainment of all the Goals. It urges actions such as lobbying governments to use sex-disaggregated data and gender-sensitive indicators (and provides information on where such indicators can be found), and pushing for a gender review process of country Millennium Development Reports. There are a number of links provided to relevant organisations, papers and tools, for further action.

Gender Equality and the Millennium Development Goals (2003), MDGenderNet

www.mdgender.net

www.mdgender.net/upload/tools/MDGender_leaflet.pdf

This brief leaflet summarises why gender equality and the empowerment of women are crucial in achieving all eight Millennium Development Goals. It provides examples of broad-based actions that would help incorporate gender equality into the Goals and result in development gains that would support the achievement of all the MDGs.

Gender Equality and the Millennium Development Goals Poster (2003), MDGenderNet

www.mdgender.net/resources/tool_detail.php?ToolID=3

Downloadable poster stating '189 Heads of States committed to Gender Equality and the Empowerment of Women. Gender equality is central to all the Millennium Development Goals'.

Organisations

Women's International Coalition for Economic Justice (WICEJ), 12 Dongan Place #206, New York, NY 10040, USA

info@wicej.org

www.wicej.org

WICEJ is an international coalition representing organisations in all regions of the globe. It works to link gender with macro-economic policy in international intergovernment policy-making arenas, from a human rights perspective. WICEJ uses an integrated feminist analysis which links the multiplicity of systems that oppress women, and recognises the diversity of women's experience by race, ethnicity, class, national origin, citizenship status, and other factors. It seeks to bring local perspectives on gender and economic issues to the international arena, and shared analysis from the international arena back to regions and national communities.

Women's Environment and Development Organization (WEDO), 355 Lexington Avenue, 3rd Floor, New York, NY 10017-6603, USA
wedo@wedo.org
www.wedo.org

Established in 1990, WEDO is an international advocacy network that seeks to increase the power of women worldwide as policy makers in governance and in policy-making institutions, forums, and processes, at all levels, to achieve economic and social justice, a peaceful and healthy planet, and human rights for all. WEDO's programme areas are Gender and Governance, Sustainable Development, and Economic and Social Justice. WEDO seeks to advocate women's equality in economic and political decision-making, find development solutions that are sustainable for women, communities, and the planet, promote economic equity for women, and increase public awareness about the negative impacts of globalisation on women, their families and their communities, and the environment.

United Nations Development Fund for Women (UNIFEM), 304 E45th Street, 15th Floor, New York, NY 10017, USA
www.unifem.org

UNIFEM is the women's fund at the UN. It was created in 1976 and provides financial and technical assistance to innovative programmes and strategies that promote women's human rights, political partici-pation, and economic security. Within the UN system, UNIFEM promotes gender equality and links women's issues and concerns to national, regional, and global agendas by fostering collaboration and providing technical expertise on gender mainstreaming and women's empowerment strategies.

Gender and Development Network (GADN), c/o WOMANKIND Worldwide, 2nd Floor, Development House, 56–64 Leonard Street, London EC2A 4JX, UK
info@gadnetwork.org.uk
www.gadnetwork.org.uk/

The GADN is a membership network of over 180 practitioners, academics, and consultants working on gender and development issues in the UK. It has been active in advocacy and awareness-raising on gender and development issues since its founding in 1985. The Network enables its members to share information and expertise, discuss concerns, lobby government and international bodies on their development programmes, and provide expert advice and comment on policies and projects. GADN members work in partnership with development and advocacy organisations throughout the world. The GADN is the UK representative for Women In Development Europe (WIDE) in Brussels.

Women In Development Europe (WIDE), rue de la Science 10, 1000 Brussels, Belgium
info@wide-network.org
www.eurosur.org/wide/home.htm

WIDE is a European network of development NGOs, gender specialists, and human rights activists. It monitors and influences international economic and development policy and practice from a feminist perspective. WIDE's work is grounded on women's rights as the basis for the development of a more just and democratic world order. WIDE strives for a world based on gender equality and social justice that ensures equal rights for all, as well as equal access to resources and opportunities in all spheres of political, social, and economic life.

International Women's Rights Action Watch – Asia Pacific (IWRAW Asia Pacific), 2nd Floor, Block F, Anjung Felda, Jalan Maktab, 54000 Kuala Lumpur, Malaysia
iwraw-ap@iwraw-ap.org
www.iwraw-ap.org/

IWRAW Asia Pacific is a non-profit international women's organisation based in the South. It promotes the domestic implementation of international human rights standards by building the capacity of women and human rights advocates to claim and realise women's human rights. This is done through the development of new knowledge and the utilisation of a rights-based approach. IWRAW Asia Pacific contributes to the progressive interpretation, universalisation, implementation, and realisation of women's human rights through the lens of CEDAW and other international human rights treaties.

WOMANKIND Worldwide, 2nd Floor, Development House, 56–64 Leonard Street, London EC2A 4JX, UK
info@womankind.org.uk
www.womankind.org.uk

WOMANKIND Worldwide is a UK-based charity dedicated to women's development and women's human rights globally. WOMANKIND Worldwide has developed programmes in partnership with local community groups to tackle women's inequality in many of the world's poorest places. These programmes are called the Four Literacies – Word Literacy, Money Literacy, Body Literacy, and Civil Literacy. WOMANKIND works to unlock women's potential and maximise their ability to make decisions in their own lives, the lives of their families, as well as in the future of their community and country. WOMANKIND Worldwide works with 70 partner organisations in 20 countries, spanning Africa, South Asia, Central and South America, and Europe.

The UN Millennium Project Task Force 3 on Primary Education and Gender Equality, Center for Global Development, 1776 Massachusetts Avenue, NW, Washington DC 20036, USA
tf3info@unmillenniumproject.org
www.unmillenniumproject.org/html/tforce_3.shtm

The UN Millennium Project Task Force has been tasked with developing an operational framework of action for meeting MDG Target 3 – to ensure that, by 2015, children everywhere, boys and girls alike, will be able to complete a full course of primary schooling. In addition, the Task Force is also developing an operational framework of action to meet MDG 3: promote gender equality and empower women. The Task Force comprises two groups (on education and gender) that will produce two separate reports, though the groups work closely together. The education group is systematically analysing the means to achieve dramatic improvements in education in the developing world, and to highlight priority actions for both developing and developed countries. The gender group has taken a broad look at the goal of gender empowerment within the framework of enhancing women's capabilities, opportunities, and security in order to meet the goal. The group is highlighting priority areas of action, which include and go beyond the issue of gender disparity in education. The Task Force has completed its Interim Reports on Education and Gender and will prepare its Final Reports by the end of 2004.

Printed in the United Kingdom
by Lightning Source UK Ltd.
131562UK00001B/167-184/A